Engaged!

A Devotional to Help a Bride-to-Be Navigate down the Aisle

• • •

Sandy Lovern

Birmingham, Alabama

New Hope® Publishers
P. O. Box 12065
Birmingham, AL 35202-2065
www.newhopepublishers.com

Library of Congress Cataloging-in-Publication Data

Lovern, Sandy, 1952-
Engaged! : a devotional to help a bride-to-be navigate down the aisle / Sandy Lovern.
p. cm.
ISBN 1-59669-035-6 (jacketed hard cover)
1. Wives—Religious life. 2. Christian women—Religious life. 3. Marriage—Religious aspects—Christianity. 4. Betrothal—Religious aspects—Christianity. 5. Weddings. I. Title.
BV4528.15.L68 2006
242'.64323—dc22
2006012458

ISBN: 1-59669-035-6
ISBN: 978-1-59669-035-6

N064150 • 1006 • 5M1

With Love

to

My Lord, who completes me, because without Him,
I have no idea who I am;

Ralph, who was always there through the
best and worst of times
and still leaves me breathlessly in love;

Jeff, whose zest for life and tenacity
constantly challenges me;

Trish, whose effervescent happiness
is my sweet inspiration;

and

Biz, who faithfully never left my side.

Table of Contents

• Week One •

• Week Two •

• WEEK THREE •

• WEEK FOUR •

• Week Five •

• Week Six •

• Week Seven •

• Week Eight •

• Week Nine •

• Week Ten •

• Week Eleven •

• Week Twelve •

Introduction

Wow! You're engaged! Can you believe it? You've been waiting for this since your childhood days when you played dress-up with your girlfriends, donned make-believe veils, and tripped down the driveway in your mom's old heels.

If you are like many engaged women, you are excited, maybe a little nervous, and your wedding planner is permanently attached to your right hand. Let me—just for a moment—gently pry that planner from your hand and urge you to take up this book. You are beginning a very complicated and challenging process, but this devotional can be a tool to bring you inspiration and guidance during this very complex time.

Before your wedding, you will be deluged with decisions, uncertainty, and emotions so raw you feel like a sushi bar that's been picked over. Imagine the peace you can experience if you take five or ten minutes each day to enter that holy place before the Lord, sit at His feet, and let Him speak to you. You can't possibly leave His presence without carrying His wise counsel, forgiveness, and love on your person. The residue of heaven is imprinted on your soul and spirit as you leave His throne of grace.

How to Use This Book

As the tension mounts, and it will, this devotional can be used at your discretion. It was written for a 12-week period, but it is not a structured step-by-step plan. You may do the devotions in order from beginning to end during your daily devotion times, or you may skip around, choosing the entry that best fits your needs for the

day. You may want to read it all the way through for inspiration, or you might need a little more time to digest each daily thought and prayer. Space is provided for you to write your own thoughts and feelings as journal entries. Years from now, you will be able to look back at what you have written and relive this special time in your life.

The engagement period can take you through an enormous range of emotions that, undirected, can quickly turn a joyous occasion into a chaotic free-for-all. This devotional shines the spotlight on you, the bride, but also illuminates all of the relationships in your life that will dramatically change. It gives you insight into the feelings of those around you from the perspective of your mate, mother, father, siblings, and friends. Mom may be giving you hives, Dad may be remote, and your chosen mate may seem to be bored already with all the wedding details—and you still have months to go. Set aside a few minutes of your day to get spiritually centered so you can hear the voice of God. He has a lot to say to brides, and only He knows what you will face each day. Through gentle moments of communion with Him, you will find the way to handle each delicate situation.

Why Did I Write This Book?

I first realized the need for this book after experiencing my own daughter's engagement period. We found that with prayer and the application of biblical principles, it was possible for us to actually stay friends, help one another, and experience together a beautiful time in her life. Of course, I'm sure it helped when I told her that this was one time in her life when she, as the bride, could actually override her mom. She loved that! The wedding was beautiful.

God has given me a tremendous passion to minister to those in love, and I have helped many young women through the joys and difficulties of engagement. It *is* possible to keep your gorgeous smile throughout the whole thing, but only with the strength you will find from the Lord. Forget about all the horror stories you've heard about brides out of control. Under the tutelage of the Lord, you are going to be one bride who calmly makes choices, takes time to remember romance, and luxuriates in this special time.

After 33 years of my own wedded bliss, I'm here to tell you it is attainable. I still get excited when I see my mate walk through the

door. How about that! I defy every statistic and poll taken today. The Bible tells us that "a three-stranded cord is not easily broken," so recognize the Lord's place in your marriage and hold on to His promises. I wrote this devotional to bring you hope and the fundamental truths of God's Word. I want to encourage you to pour all of yourself into this marriage commitment, and you will never run dry. Apply His principles in your marriage, and you will never be shaken. Give the Lord priority in your life, and His face will always shine upon you.

Week One

• *Wedding Tips* •

Checklist: Get ideas for the wedding cake and wedding favors. Rent men's formal wear. Hire wedding day transportation. Give your guest list to shower hostess, and start your wedding registries before shower invitations are sent. Reserve rental equipment.

• • •

Make several labeled folders: flowers, table arrangements, gift ideas, wedding cakes, hot new ideas, etc. As you read the bridal magazines, cut out the pictures and ideas that you like and file them. Nothing is worse than trying to go back through tons of magazines to find that one picture of that purse you thought was so cute.

• • •

Checklist: Get passports if necessary. Order wedding rings. Confirm that your bridesmaids have ordered their gowns, and decide on bridal accessories. Discuss menu ideas with caterer. Order the wedding cake. Choose the invitations, and check on proper wording etiquette.

DAY 1

So Now You're Engaged

A little girl's dream is now a woman's reality.

Thou wilt shew me the path of life:
in thy presence is fullness of joy; at thy right hand
there are pleasures for evermore.

—Psalm 16:11

Finally, it happened. Eeeeeeeeeeeeeeeeeeeeeee!

All those years of dressing up Barbie dolls and donning make-believe veils made from Mom's old tablecloths have culminated into this moment. The man of your dreams has asked you to be his wife, and joy is surging through you. Suddenly, hundreds of doors have opened, and your life has exploded into numerous diverse directions. You are evolving into someone's soul mate, wife, domestic engineer, interior decorator, chef…and the doors keep opening.

Let's stay in this moment and savor the happiness. The sun is brighter, the wind is crisper, and everything is perfect. You want the world to stop and listen to you for a second. "Hey everyone, he loves me and has asked me to be his bride." I mean, what could possibly be more important in the whole wide world than that?

You are experiencing pure joy, the kind that bubbles up inside of you and overshadows everything. Joy is a tremendous spiritual

force wherein anything becomes possible. Your heart expands and your soul soars so high that, for a short time, you ride upon the winds in heavenly realms. Now I know your thoughts are bubbling with frothy wedding gowns, guest lists, creamy roses, and luscious lemon wedding cakes, but right now, if you listen very quietly, you can hear the voice of God. Take a moment to thank Him for giving you a mate, someone with whom you can build a future.

Father, *thank You for watching over me all these years and preparing me for this wonderful mate. Help me hold on to this special moment, and over the years, when there are days in which the luster of marriage has grown dim, give me the gift of remembrance. Take me back to this day when You gave me everything I ever dreamed of. May I never lose this joy.*

JOYFUL THOUGHTS

DAY 2

ARE YOU SURE HE'S THE ONE?

Remember he's nonrefundable.

During the forty years that I led you through the desert,
your clothes did not wear out, nor did the sandals on your feet.
You ate no bread and drank no wine or other fermented drink.
I did this so that you might know that I am the LORD *your God.*

—Deuteronomy 29:5–6 (NIV)

Selecting your lifelong mate is not like purchasing a new pair of shoes. The Lord wants the best for you, so this is one time in your life when you avoid "the clearance rack," "markdowns," and "knockoffs." Shopping provides options. If you decide you don't like something, you return it for a refund, or if you change your mind about that impulse item you bought while shopping with the girls, back it goes. However, your man is nonrefundable. That's why prior to saying, "I do," you need to make sure the Lord isn't saying, "Don't."

Well, how do you do that? Now is the time to *stop* if you made your decision to marry based on any of the following: feeling boxed in, pressured by peers, your internal clock, or any other emotion besides love. You don't want to experience buyer's remorse. Marriage is not a bargain-basement free-for-all sale. It is a choice that will cost you dearly. The price? Your entire life. So how do you make wise choices?

If I said you could buy only one pair of shoes and they had to last you 40 years, I bet you would bypass those dangerous "to die for" stilettos and those painful "too cute" Mary Janes. See how quickly you changed directions? It's all about making good choices based on long-term plans. I feel certain you would be looking for shoes based on specific criteria, such as durability, integrity of the manufacturer, what they are made of, how they perform under constant use, and how well they protect your feet.

Now, apply similar criteria when choosing a mate. Character endures over the years; fads fade. The important factors are not how gorgeous he is or what sort of men are in style today. Rather, consider how he is under pressure, what he is made of, whether he is dependable, and what his family is like. There are no guarantees with any decision except your salvation, but with the Lord's help, you can be guided in the right direction. If you find you have made an error in promising to marry him, that's OK. Just love him enough to let him go so he can find that perfect woman the Lord has for him.

Father, *Your Word assures me there is safety in a multitude of counsel. I ask You to confirm whether or not this is the man You have for me. Send me wise counsel, and open my ears to hear it. Quiet the raging storm of indecision inside of me, and give me peace, as You confirm in my heart that I have done Your perfect will.*

THOUGHTS OF ASSURANCE AND WISDOM

3 DAY

COMMITMENT

This is not a girly popcorn-and-pj's sleepover.

And he charged them, saying, Thus shall ye do in the fear of the LORD, faithfully, and with a perfect heart.
—2 Chronicles 19:9

In all your life, you have never been in a relationship like the one you are about to enter into now. As you watch old movies, another hand will be dipping into the popcorn, and those old T-shirts with the holes in them will hopefully be replaced with some lacy lingerie. When you wake up each morning, Dorothy, Toto may not be cuddled up next to you, but you will be home.

In your previous relationships, you had little "escape tactics." If you got upset with one of your friends or someone in your family, you could leave, hang up, clam up, or walk away. Not so with this one. When you softly said, "Yes," and he placed that sparkling diamond ring upon your finger, you unleashed a whole lot of promises. That man looked into your eyes and asked you to spend the rest of your life with him. There weren't any "what if's," "but's," or "how about's." You both must make a through-thick-and-thin commitment from the heart, an unbreakable agreement that

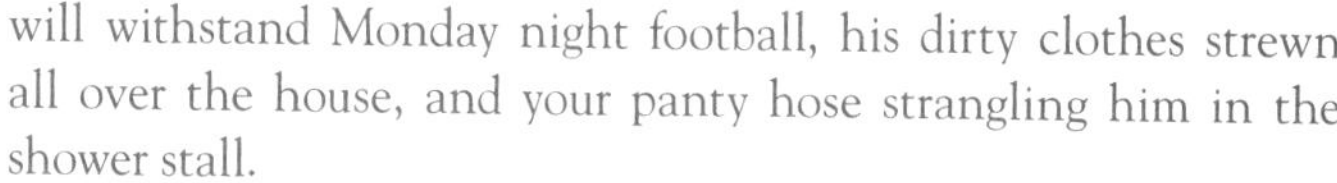

will withstand Monday night football, his dirty clothes strewn all over the house, and your panty hose strangling him in the shower stall.

The Lord is the best example you will ever have of someone who exemplifies the term *commitment*. He is faithful no matter what you have done, are doing, or will do. Why? Because He has unconditional love for you. Lay aside all the requirements we, as a people, put on having a relationship with Him, and you will find that all He wants is your love. The bottom line is this: if you and your mate focus on your love, all the other little inconveniences and irritations of life will flutter to the ground as gently as a rose sheds its beautiful petals.

Commitment has become a scary word because it is so powerful and all encompassing. When you asked the Lord to come into your heart, you entered into a relationship that will last throughout eternity. He brought you a sense of security and steadfastness that lets you know, no matter what occurs in life, you have a friend.

So make a double batch of popcorn, hang those panty hose in the laundry room, and buy a great big hamper, because your mate, your new best friend, just wants to hang out, relax, and enjoy the journey through life with you!

Father, *thank You for believing in me. Help me to be a woman of integrity and steadfastness. Show me how to be faithful, as You are, and let my life reflect Your attributes. I want to be a woman of honor, determination, and courage.*

DAY 4

HEAVEN'S APPROVAL

Has the Lord RSVP'd yet?

"Do not work for food that spoils, but for food that endures to eternal life, which the Son of Man will give you. On him God the Father has placed his seal of approval."

—John 6:27 (NIV)

In our society, it is considered a sign of respect when a man asks for the blessings of his future bride's parents. How much more should you seek the approval of your heavenly Father, simply because you love and respect Him!

If you have gotten all caught up in the hullabaloo surrounding your wedding and forgot to seek the heart of God, do it today. Better yet, have you asked your Father to actually participate in the planning of your affair? Turn your wedding over to Him. Allow Him to orchestrate it, and you will see tiny miracles throughout the entire planning process.

Your heavenly Father has watched you grow and mature into a beautiful woman. You are His daughter, and He wants to walk you down the aisle, have your hand resting upon His arm, waltz you across the floor, and see your joy as you stand nestled in the arms of your husband. Make sure He is included in every aspect of your wedding, and He will make your day perfect.

The key is to make sure you have His approval. "How do I do that?" you might ask. You will find His heart and His will when you go to Him on your knees. It really is no great mystery or mystical experience. Remember how you sought the approval of your mom or dad when you were a child? When you received it, it was not always accompanied with a verbal response, but it always brought an "inward knowing" you had made them proud by the choices you had made. So it is with the Lord.

He will give you small signs along the way. His approval will be felt in many ways, such as, peace amidst wedding confusion, an enlarged capacity for compromise, small snafus suddenly fixed, relationships miraculously mended, and dreams made into realities. As for an RSVP from the Lord, invite Him...He'll come!

Father, *today I turn this whole wedding over to You. Forgive me if in any way I have excluded You from one of the most important events in my life. Thank You for Your miraculous presence. Keep Your hand upon me, please. I am grateful You are here to walk with me through this wonderful time in my life. Let me know whether my plans have Your approval, and may Your face shine upon me and my mate all the days of our lives.*

DAY 5

BE OF GOOD CHEER

Your Romeo is here.

He brought me to the banqueting house,
and his banner over me was love.
—Song of Solomon 2:4

So you are engaged! Is your head still spinning? No more plucking daisies, "He loves me. He loves me not." He most certainly does love you, and that sparkling promise encircling your finger is proof. Now that the news of your engagement has been broadcast over a thousand cell phones and your friends have shrieked enough to raise the nation's security level, let's get down to the good stuff.

The dress…ah, the dress! Visions of frothy lace, creamy chiffon confections, and buttery satin gowns drift through your mind. Will you choose sleek and elegant? Or maybe layer upon layer of lace? Or how about a billowing Cinderella gown? So many options—and the choices are all yours to make.

Prepare yourself to deal with some astonishing emotions, because this shopping trip will be like no other in your life. You might want to bring an extra hankie for your mom, because she will be impacted by this day as much as you will. Mom is probably

going to have a glazed look on her face when she sees her pigtailed baby gracefully standing fully attired in a filmy veil and shimmering dress. She is not zoning out; she's just traversing back in time and seeing images from your birth to this moment. She's comparing your elegant neck with her baby's dimply one, your delicate hands with her baby's chubby fists, and your lovely face with her toddler's face, which was so often smeared with strawberry jam. Here's the moment—quick, grab it—don't miss it. This is the rite of passage. Suddenly, like an atom splitting, as the eyes of you and your mom meet in the mirror, a woman is born…and it's you!

Ah, Juliet, Juliet, be of good cheer for your Romeo awaits you. Look in the mirror at the beautiful woman you have become, and take a moment to really see the work of God's hands. His spirit birthed in you everything you are or could ever hope to be. You truly are the work of His hands, and what a fine job He has done!

Today, take time to marvel and rejoice in the power of the Lord. He has molded a clay vessel into an exquisite work of art—a woman.

Father, *thank You for never giving up on me. You have nurtured me all these years, and I choose this day to delight in who I am. Give me the self-confidence to walk in all You have for me. I ask for Your grace and the ability to see the beauty that lies hidden in my own heart. Of those who cross my path, let my eyes see past their flesh, and allow me to see the wonder that resides in each one.*

Cheerful Thoughts

· DAY 6 ·

Changing the Personal Pronouns

It's time to change the "I" to "we"— and the "me" to "us."

Give instruction to a wise man, and he will be yet wiser: teach a just man, and he will increase in learning.

—Proverbs 9:9

With all you have to do, can you believe that you really need to take time for a lesson in grammar? You must relearn the terms *singular* and *plural*. Did you know you've been pluralized? When you said, "I will marry you," you became a plural and innocently agreed to fuse your life with another.

After you have striven so many years to become an independent woman, blazing your own trails, you now have to reach back into your youth and drag forth that infernal verb *share, which* you constantly heard as a child.

Those items you have called my car, my camera, and my TV have instantly been given a different possessive pronoun and become our car, our camera, and our TV. Your conversation, consisting of "I'm going on vacation," "I'm buying a new car," and "I want this adorable puppy I saw," has now been parlayed into "We're going on vacation," "We're buying a new car," and, hopefully, "We're getting a new puppy."

It may appear you are losing some independence and a whole lot of possessions, but in reality, you are gaining so much more. Now you will have two cars, two cameras, and, if you smile real sweetly, maybe an adorable new puppy you both can potty train. Marriage is not only about sharing your heart—real issues of possessions and passions will need to be dealt with. Some persons may say these things are not important, but in reality, they are. If you think you will never run into this problem, just wait until you climb into your cute little sports car and he has moved your seat back, adjusted your rearview mirror, and messed up all your preset radio stations.

Remember, we are now sharing! He is going to have a lot of adjustments also. How do you think he is going to feel when you schedule an appointment at the florist for the two of you at a time he planned on watching a golf tournament? How is he going to take it when you use his best jersey as a nightie? Yet with all the adjustments that will be necessary, it is a wise woman who learns how truly blessed she is to have a mate to share her life. Think about it: now you will have someone to get up at 4 A.M. to walk that sweet puppy!

Father, *I know Your Word tells me out of the abundance of the heart, the mouth speaks. Help me make this transition from thinking "It's all about me" to realizing "It's all about us." I desire to share my life, my possessions, and my heart with the man I love.*

DAY 7

Take Him as He Is

Your prince changeth not.

Train up a child in the way he should go:
and when he is old, he will not depart from it.
—Proverbs 22:6

Get a picture of your future intended when he was a child and study it very carefully. Do you see that mischievous, toothless, smiling little boy? Do you see him in that dirty T-shirt, which is hanging over those baggy jeans, which, in turn, are draped over those untied sneakers? Well, that's the responsible young man you promised to live your life with. Don't fool yourself into thinking that little boy has gone anywhere. He is masquerading in a conservative button-down collar shirt and well-trimmed locks. He is still there, hiding behind that gorgeous smile.

Talk to his parents, siblings, and relatives. Those antics he pulled as a child, like putting bubble gum in his sister's hair and booby-trapping the house with firecrackers, were all signs of who he really is. Maybe those who know him will relate stories of how he spent hours by himself playing with his erector set and reading comic books. It could be that he spent his days

catching tadpoles and digging up the front yard, looking for fishing worms.

Your young man today is comprised of everything he ever was. Brick upon brick, line upon line, he has developed into the man you love, and believe me, he changeth not. If he was a Dennis the Menace clone as a child, be prepared to live a life of surprises and mishaps. Perhaps he loved reading for hours; then you can expect this man to want a lot of time alone. If he loved bugs and digging in the dirt with play trucks, you may have yourself an outdoorsman who loves sports. If he was stubborn as a child—*hello*—then this is one mule you won't budge. If he was an overachiever, prepare yourself for a life that will constantly be changing. Maybe he loved painting or writing; then you have a creative one whose emotions run deep.

Don't think that somehow your presence in his life is going to change the very makeup of who he is, because you will only become frustrated. In other words, what you see is what you get, and remember, that is what you love about him. Now if you can accept him under these terms, exactly as he is today, then you're on the right track.

Look at that picture one more time, because he comes as a package deal, all those freckles included.

Father, *thank You for making my mate who he is. Let wisdom guide me this day, and let my love be expansive enough to accommodate all he really is inside. Help him to trust me enough to be himself, with no facades. I want to be a part of making all his dreams and aspirations come true.*

THOUGHTS OF MY MATE AS A CHILD

WEEK TWO

• *Wedding Tip* •

Get a piece of poster board, and on it, coordinate your wedding to make sure that your ideas flow and colors blend visually. On the board, put swatches of material from your bridesmaid dresses; a close-up picture of the embellishments on your gown; and pictures of your centerpieces, flowers, bridal bouquet, or other relevant decorations. Carry the board with you wherever you go to assist you in matching bridal jewelry, program paper, lighting, or whatever comes up.

• DAY 8 •

The Power of Laughter

Sometimes it's all there is.

A merry heart doeth good like a medicine:
but a broken spirit drieth the bones.
—Proverbs 17:22

If you have the gift of being able to laugh at yourself, then you will sail through this whole wedding process. Can't quite see your life as an enactment of the Three Stooges? Then you have the next three months to cultivate a great sense of humor. Laughter is an effective and wonderful antidote for stress.

When David said, "Praise the LORD, O my soul" (Psalm 146:1), he was actually taking control of his soul and dictating his emotions. So is Auntie Mabel adamant about wearing that outlandish orange dress? Laugh about it. Let's face it—you have two choices: You can either allow minor problems to have power over you and your emotions, or you can take charge of the situation with laughter. If you can chuckle over a problem, that immediately releases any emotional hold the problem has over you and restores you to a position of power.

Later on in your marriage, the ability to laugh over circumstances will carry you through many difficult situations. In the

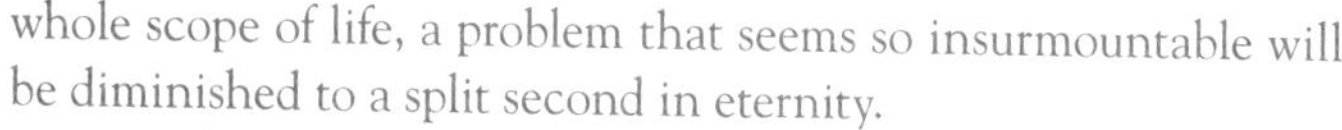

whole scope of life, a problem that seems so insurmountable will be diminished to a split second in eternity.

Besides all of the practical reasons for laughter, it also provides hidden blessings. Laughter will make your eyes sparkle and your skin glow...and save you a ton of money on miracle face creams. It's generally believed that it takes more muscles to frown than it does to smile, and studies indicate that happy people live longer. Watch children for a while. Kids giggle at puppies and hoot at the strange faces we make for them. The persuasive power of a smile is priceless. How can anyone resist a bride who is happy and smiling?

You see, people are watching you, even when you don't know it. All that tooth whitener you've been using is serving a good purpose. It's not just to look great in your wedding photos; it's to flash that beautiful smile you have and brighten someone else's day.

Father, *make me an instrument of happiness. Give me the gift of holy laughter, and show me how to use its medicinal benefits for others around me who are lacking joy in their lives. Let my eyes, the windows of my soul, sparkle with merriment and my mouth speak words of encouragement to someone who needs it.*

DAY 9

THE ULTIMATE FRIENDSHIP

Through PMS and debt, he'll be there.

A man that hath friends must shew himself friendly:
and there is a friend that sticketh closer than a brother.
—Proverbs 18:24

You have friends who have stuck with you through thick and thin, and you treasure those relationships, but now you are entering into another realm of friendship. This friendship has the capacity to go so deep that you actually lose yourself in another person and the intensity to lift you so high that nothing becomes unreachable. This is possible because someone is supporting you, allowing you to stand on his shoulders.

The difference between relationships with your friends and the relationship with your mate is that your friends have their own lives—they're on another road—but you and your mate are traveling together on a path the Lord has designed for you two alone. Your traveling buddy will be there when you need to stop and take a breather in life. He will support you when you stumble and carry you if you get too weak to go on.

You have heard it said that men refuse to ask for directions, and that is generally so true. Picture your life together as a giant

road trip. When you are PMSing, your mate is totally confused and lost, but don't think he is going to stop and ask for directions. No, he's going to wear himself out, going around and around in the same place until finally your emotional outbursts make him park that overheated car, which is all he knows to do, and wait for the engine to cool down.

You both will run into gridlocks, where life seems to stand still and frustrations turn into road rage. Then, there may be times when you can't move forward because you are so broke you can't even pay the tollbooth operator. What do you do? You make a U-turn and take the long way around life. The good news is that instead of whizzing through life, you get to take a leisurely drive through the beautiful countryside. You both will eventually get where you're going, and you'll have explored the exciting things in life together. At the end of your journey, it will be your sweet husband, your best friend, who will be with you to remind you of all the zany mishaps and special moments you have shared. So pack up, grab that wedding planner, and hang on for the ride of your life!

Father, *thank You for my wonderful friend. Teach me to value his friendship and to realize the potential we have together. Your Word tells me a three-stranded cord is not easily broken, and I trust You to be that all-important third strand in our cord. You're the potter and I am the clay, so please mold me into Your image of what a friend should be. I pray for those who need a friend today. Please send someone to brighten their day.*

THOUGHTS OF MY BEST FRIEND

DAY 10

HAVE A VISION GREATER THAN YOURSELVES

Word paint a dream.

For the vision is yet for an appointed time, but at the end it shall speak, and not lie: though it tarry, wait for it; because it will surely come, it will not tarry.

—Habakkuk 2:3

One of the quickest ways to dispel your stress and worry is to take a few minutes and think about something else besides what is going on in the immediate moment. As long as you stay in the moment, you feel the effects of what is happening, but when you think about the next hour, day, or week, you are freed up to dream. The Lord said He always provides a way of escape, and here is one for you.

Get a vision of what He has planned for your life. Set your eyes on the goal, not on the stumbling blocks along the way. Your wedding day is a monumental step in your life, but it is only one of many steps. You have already set your plans in motion, and one way or the other, you will wed the man of your dreams. It may not be sunny outside, the cake may look like the leaning Tower of Pisa, and Grandpa may shimmy all over the dance floor, but you will get married. Now that we have established that your marriage is a given under *any* circumstances, let's move forward in time.

Take a moment and look past your wedding day. What do you see? Oh! There is a rainbow after the wedding shower! There will be lazy, relaxing days, just chilling with your best friend: quiet mornings peeping at each other over the morning paper, sipping your caffe latte, with the whole beautiful day stretching out before you. There is the exciting prospect of what you will accomplish together—under the direction of the Lord.

What do you envision the two of you doing? Do you two feel a passion for any particular causes? Do the homeless tug at your hearts, or do the elderly remind you of your dear old grandma? The Lord has a specific plan tailored for your lives, and He wants to use you as His servants in a world that is in dire need of compassion, hope, and joy. Conceive a dream as to how you two will serve, and word paint that dream.

What do I mean by "word paint a dream"? Aside from your careers, you need an outlet to let the gospel flow out of you. You will know what direction you are led by the gifts you possess. Verbally acknowledge your vision by saying what you want to accomplish for the Lord. Then, as with a coloring book, fill in those words with works toward your goal!

Father, *I want our union to accomplish many things. Take us beyond our own vision, and help us see through Your eyes the needs of those around us. May our lives be presented to You as a living canvas, depicting a dream that was painted with kindness, compassion, and love. I pray You hear the cries of so many who are in need today.*

Thoughts of What Our Life Can Be— My Vision

DAY 11

ROMANCE

Keep the butterflies fluttering.

The voice of my beloved! behold,
he cometh leaping upon the mountains,
skipping upon the hills.
—Song of Solomon 2:8

Love is an intangible thing, but its attributes can be seen in a beautiful butterfly. What is it about butterflies that makes us stop in our tracks to observe them, generates giggles in children, and causes puppies to roll head over heels as they chase them?

The attraction is their beauty as they dance, their freedom, and their ability to evoke happy emotions in us. Romance in a relationship can be described as the wonderful feelings we have sans heavy words like commitment and responsibility. It's the sparkly bow on the package that holds love. It is love that is as delicate as a butterfly's brush against your cheek and is comprised of crystal moments, soft touches, and words as sweet as honey.

Romance adorns love like rosettes on a cake or those drop-dead gorgeous earrings with that little black dress. It's the zest that brings refreshment into your lives and, like the butterflies, makes you stop, look, and laugh with each other.

Don't get so overloaded with wedding details that you forget to make romance happen, and yes, you do need to activate it. It is not some magical force that plays hide-and-seek in your life; it is a mood created by you and your future mate. Learn to recognize romance. Here's a clue: it is not always neatly packaged in flowers, candy, and candlelit dinners. Romance comes disguised in actions, such as your love checking the oil in your car or handing you melted gummy bears he forgot were in his shirt pocket.

Romance is the moments you or he stopped and thought about the other. It's the anticipation of being together, and, as described in today's Scripture, it's the excitement you feel simply because you hear his voice. So remember in the coming days and the later years as you grow old together…grab hold of each other and take time to dance.

Father, *everything is always new and fresh with You. Give me the ability to dance through my life. Let my eyes recognize the sparkle with which You've adorned life, and help me to always be drawn toward Your light. I want to always have the anticipation, expectation, and wonderment of a child. May I never grow dull of hearing or weary of seeing Your miraculous creation.*

Thoughts of Romance

· DAY 12 ·

SUBMISSION OF THE HEART

It's not a heel mark on your back.

Submitting yourselves one to another in the fear of God.
—Ephesians 5:21

Do you remember playing musical chairs as a child? The one who was the quickest and pushed the most always won. While the wedding march is playing, let's not have you and your mate racing around those imaginary chairs, jockeying for position to see who is going to be the boss in your marriage. Your relationship can be a win-win situation. Submission is not "giving up"; it is opening up one's self to allow another to be accountable for part of the load. It is an act of the heart, not of the will.

Have you ever watched a duck with her babies? She is definitely the authority and is responsible for providing food and a home for her little ones. When food is found, she steps back and allows the babies to eat. There is no question she is the boss, and she could eat all the food herself; but as a mother, she submits to the needs of her babies. You and your mate will learn to submit to each other, caring for the other's needs as if

they were your own. You will use all your strengths for the sake of the family you have become—not as a way of being the boss.

Both of you have strengths, so wisely make the most of them. If your intended is skilled in finances, then leave that task to him. If you have more people skills, then when it's time to wheel and deal for a new car, it might be better if your intended submits his predatory desire for the "hunt" and lets you do the car buying.

The problem with musical chairs is that when the music stops and you are nestled in that one remaining chair, you are in the hot seat to accomplish exactly what you said you could and would do. If you told your intended not to worry because you would pick out the music for the wedding, and then the band doesn't show up or ends up playing Guy Lombardo music all night long, you can't blame him. You accepted the task, and even though he really wanted Jimmy Buffet and snare drums, he entrusted it to you.

Now, let's make one point about submission perfectly clear: submission does not make you a doormat, and the only heel marks that should be on your back ought to be from him trying to walk out the kinks you've developed from all the prewedding stress!

Father, *please give me a pliable heart and will when it comes to sharing responsibilities. Show me how to pick and choose my battles and overcome any compulsion I have to do it all myself. Let this perfection I strive for begin with perfecting myself in You. Help me to own the words, "Just let it go," when things don't always go my way.*

THOUGHTS OF OUR STRENGTHS

· DAY 13 ·

HEADING IN THE SAME DIRECTION

U-turns are not allowed.

And the LORD said, Behold, the people is one, and they have all one language; and this they begin to do: and now nothing will be restrained from them, which they have imagined to do.

—Genesis 11:6

You're heading out to check on hotel reservations for your wedding guests, and your intended is heading toward the couch to watch a basketball game. What do you do? How about nothing? That's right. Remember, yesterday you prayed to own the words, "Just let it go." What can you possibly hope to achieve by arguing, demanding, or stamping your pedicured little foot?

If he is forced to go with you, he will be mad about missing the game, both of you will silently smolder in the car, and your mind will tell you he doesn't really care. At that point, the two of you will not be traveling in the same direction. In fact, he probably will have already taken a U-turn and ended up back there on the basketball court. Hotel reservations? As far as he is concerned, a bunch of sleeping bags would do just fine. Men don't think along the same lines as women do, so what's the point of getting all worked up?

If you want to travel in the same direction, meet up with one of your friends, have lunch, book those hotel rooms, and make

plans to meet your intended after his game. It may not be fair, nor is it "even," but did you get to where you were going? Are the rooms booked? Traveling in the same direction means moving forward together, not backward. Along some of the miles of life, you will be driving while he catnaps, and for other miles, he will be at the wheel while you doze off. It's this division of energy that will make the two of you a very powerful team.

To head in the same direction, develop a tag-team mentality. If you both ran at your top speed all the time, you'd only be able to go so far, and then both of you would have to take a break. How much better is it for you, while you are at your best and have clear direction, to take off and run with the ball? When you get tired, tag him. He loves you and desires to help. But remember, his help is probably not going to be exactly the way you imagined it or would choose it to be. Once you tag him and he's headed down the road, just watch him go and let him do it his way. If you both are clear as to what you have established as your finish line, then whatever you imagined as your goal, you will achieve. How you get there doesn't really matter, does it?

Father, *when I got engaged I had certain visions of how I wanted my wedding to be. Give me grace to recognize my intended has no idea what my vision is and, therefore, has no way of understanding what I want to accomplish. Let me be a different kind of bride-to-be—let me be remembered for my cheerful attitude and my ability to cross the finish line with a smile on my face, holding the hand of the one I love.*

Thoughts on Going in the Same Direction

DAY 14

UNDERSTANDING ONE ANOTHER

Yes, it's possible!

Give therefore thy servant an understanding heart to judge thy people, that I may discern between good and bad: for who is able to judge this thy so great a people?

—1 Kings 3:9

The definition of *understanding* is "to show a sympathetic or tolerant attitude toward something." If you have ever attended any workshops or conferences on dealing with people, one of the pat phrases they advise you to use in difficult situations is, "I understand." These words have the amazing ability to avert anger, soothe hurt feelings, and defuse explosive situations.

When you attempt to understand someone else's point of view, it increases your capacity to walk in their shoes. You may not agree, but with understanding comes temperance. Who can understand how your intended can turn his T-shirt inside out and wear it for another day, or how he can stand to sleep on sheets that haven't been washed in a month? But it's not your job to change him; it is your responsibility to try to understand him. Those things may not have the slightest bit of importance to him, and yet he may go bonkers if his CDs are not alphabetically arranged. Go figure!

In the same light, he probably doesn't get it why a woman needs to buy a new dress for every special affair she attends. All he knows is that you look great in that little sundress, so you could just throw some heels on in place of those sandals, and you're set to go.

So how do you meet in the middle and still understand where the other is coming from? Surprisingly enough, the secret is trust. Trust that what he does is where his comfort level is. If he becomes uncomfortable with something he does, then he will enact change. Your attempt to make him see the error of his ways is not going to work. If you both can learn the art of talking to one another, then you are on the way to understanding each other.

Question him about what you don't understand; then accept what he has to say, even though it may make no sense to you. Tell him things about yourself that he may not know. Giving each other the liberty to talk brings tremendous freedom, which results in invaluable trust.

Father, *please give me an understanding heart. I thank You for the uniqueness of my intended. I love him for who he is. Help me draw on his strengths, and let me never forget that he is a creation You fashioned. I want to be a wise woman who learns early in life the value of understanding.*

Thoughts on Understanding

WEEK THREE

• *Wedding Tips* •

Checklist: Select your music for the ceremony and reception, and meet with your musicians and singers. Look into opening joint bank accounts. Check your insurance coverage. Make your honeymoon plans, and shop for what you will need on your trip.

• • •

Today's idyllic veil material is nylon tulle because other tulle tends to become limp when damp. The fewer ornaments on your veil the better, since rhinestones, pearls, and other adornments can photograph like black dots, leaving dark spots in your photos.

Something Old, Something New, Something Borrowed, Something Blue

Nostalgia calls you home.

Lift up thine eyes round about, and behold: all these gather themselves together, and come to thee. As I live, saith the LORD, thou shalt surely clothe thee with them all, as with an ornament, and bind them on thee, as a bride doeth.

—Isaiah 49:18

As you organize your wedding, there are some things you will do that are really "up close and personal." Your fairy-tale day will be comprised of many important memories of your life, encapsulated and enacted through the familiar words, "something old, something new, something borrowed, something blue." The choosing of particular items to carry or adorn yourself with is a British custom that stems from an old nursery rhyme.

Something old represents continuity and stability; so today, take some time to reminisce. What do you possess that triggers a warm, nostalgic memory? In other words, what is an item that "takes you home" in your mind? Spiritually, you are carrying forth the deep-rooted beliefs and traditions that have made you who you are today.

Something new signifies hope or optimism for the future. This category is wide-open to have fun with and today's brides are opting for things that run the gamut from conventional jewelry to zany miracle water bras. The symbolization of something new is that you are excitedly walking into the future.

The something borrowed is said to be borrowed happiness. What item that belongs to someone you love and respect do you want to have with you on your wedding day? My daughter blessed me when she asked to borrow her father's stopwatch, because he had used it to time my contractions the day she was born. Now that will bring a few tears to anyone's eyes.

Something blue represents love, innocence, and faithfulness. This can be as unpretentious as a baby blue ribbon sewn unto your crinoline.

The whole nursery rhyme concept is that you carry on your person items that represent who you are, where you came from, and where you are going. On your wedding day, the "new" represents you walking by faith into a pristine life with your mate; the "borrowed" is that you understand you will always need the support of friends; the "old" is a reminder of your heritage; and the "blue" demonstrates your desire to be awakened from your innocence.

Father, *I thank You for sweet memories I can carry along this new road I will be traveling. I ask a blessing on my friends and family, from whom I have received so much. I loved having the innocence of a child, but I am ready to take on the responsibilities of being a wife. Help me bind these beautiful traditions in my heart.*

Thoughts of Things Old, New, Borrowed, and Blue

· DAY 16 ·

LACE, TULLE, AND TROUBLES

Overwhelmed? Go to the Rock.

From the end of the earth will I cry unto thee,
when my heart is overwhelmed: lead me to
the rock that is higher than I.

—Psalm 61:2

The continued task of planning a wedding looms large in front of you. Quite frankly, it is overwhelming. You have always dreamed of peach-colored bridesmaid dresses, but Patti wants them to be salmon-colored, and Julie prefers just a hint of melon. Can you believe there are so many shades of orange? Location is also an issue: you want a serene, relaxed outdoor site, whereas your future in-laws are championing for a stately, elegant country club atmosphere. What about the budget? You are trying to keep costs down, but who could resist that gorgeous triple-layer veil?

Unless you take control, the whole affair will mushroom overnight from a tiny mustard seed into a ten-foot-high herb. When you think you are sinking under the weight of the pressures, climb up on the Rock. Jesus has a way of gentling the situation. He can make those intimidating mountains look like little sand dunes and those raging rivers look like streams. See,

He is so huge, so grand, that when you look at Him, everything else becomes small. He can breathe upon your soul and settle things down.

When the pressures of the wedding start intruding on your joy, it is time to escape. Run—don't walk—to the Rock that is higher than you. Sometimes you may have to claw your way up (remember to be careful with those fingernails), but the view from the top is spectacular. With Jesus, you can see for miles and miles, and from there, it looks like clear sailing over the next few weeks. You may experience some turbulence, but remember, Jesus has a long reach, and He will never let you fall!

Lord, *I want to know You as the Rock. When I am overcome with decisions and it seems I have too many choices to make, I ask You to help me decipher what is really important. Let me stay sensitive to those around me who have opinions different from mine, but also help me become my own woman. Make my forehead like flint for warding off guilt and criticism. Give me insight on how special this day is for me. Today, I want to sit with You all day long on the mountaintop and just enjoy the view.*

Thoughts on Being Rock Solid

· DAY 17 ·

PREPARING THE VESSEL

The agenda's prepared.
Now how about the vessel?

So Jotham became mighty, because he prepared his ways before the LORD his God.

—2 Chronicles 27:6

Are you ready for this? The familiar, dusty old road of your life is about to divide into an eight-lane expressway. Changes, decisions, responsibilities, and exciting new challenges will be racing toward you. You must take your foot off the brake, grab hold of the wheel, and let the Lord direct you.

If you prepare, then you will be bolstered for the day. Have you ever started to make a cake only to find you didn't have the necessary ingredients because you had not prepared ahead of time? When something like that happens, what happens to you? You get irritated, and what you anticipate to be a fun project suddenly turns into a chore. So it is with life. The tiniest things can become huge if they are accompanied with frustration. As you prepare for your wedding, we don't want you turning into Bridezilla, do we?

Everyone has heard horror stories of the strange things some brides do. The horrific responses you have heard of are usually

the result of the bride running too fast, reacting versus enacting, and thinking only of herself. Take time to align your body, soul, and spirit. Load up on vitamins because your stressed body will be eating them like candy. Drink plenty of water, and rest when you can. Feed your soul with soothing music, sing praises to the Lord, and feast your eyes on the beauty around you. The Word is alive and food for your spirit, so read your Bible every day. If you feel empty, snack on the Word; it has miraculous, energizing qualities that far surpass those of a hastily eaten energy bar with the taste of oatmeal-coated cardboard.

Like an athlete, the more you train, the stronger you become. Jotham became mighty as he prepared his ways before the Lord, and so can you. Make the decision early to keep your eyes focused on the goal—fulfilling God's will for your life. A good marriage is a crucial part of that.

Today, stop for a moment and check out your alignment. Body, soul, and spirit—are they all on board and in sync with one another? Good!

Father, *help me prepare my ways this day before You. May my heart be toward You, my mind be filled with only good thoughts, and my will be pliable enough for You to direct me in the way I should go. Keep my spirit, soul, and body blameless until the coming of my Lord Jesus Christ.* And Father, please steer me away from those Snickers bars, and lead me to the greener pastures of vegetables. Thank You for giving me humor to defuse difficult situations throughout this coming day.*

*See 1 Thessalonians 5:23.

Thoughts on Preparing My Vessel

DAY 18

GOD FIRST

He needs to be seated at the head table.

Let not mercy and truth forsake thee: bind them about thy neck; write them upon the table of thine heart.

—Proverbs 3:3

You have many ideas for your wedding theme streaming through your mind, and I bet your forehead is the only spot around that doesn't have a sticky note attached. The guest list should be ready by now, and you'll want to double-check to make sure the Lord is seated at the head of your table, the table of your heart. If you want your ideas to flow effortlessly, your mind to be crystal clear, and your attitude to be one of sublime peace, then you must give Him precedence in all you do.

It is really very simple and only takes a split second to get His approval for each thing you do. Make your life a continual prayer by talking with Him all day long. You'd be surprised at how much He wants to be involved in your wedding plans. When it comes to picking out flowers, He is the Master of color and hue. He has already chosen the officiant for your wedding, the one He wants to bless your union. But God is patience personified, and He will quietly *wait* for you to ask His opinion.

The world turns to psychics and tarot card readers; we turn to the Lord, who knows all that was, is, and is to come. If you want to know if your guests are going to like the menu you've chosen, ask Him. The Lord will point out any problems you might have overlooked, and He will remind you about Uncle Harry's allergy to salmon, which you totally forgot.

Now, don't think His answers will come blaring out of that dried-up fern sitting on your desk. There won't be any burning bushes, because these days, we have fire extinguishers. His answers are the gentle thoughts that blow through your mind like a cool wind—the ones that cause you to think, *Ahhhhhhhhhhh, what a good idea! Why didn't I think of that?* Or you might be worried about your wedding finances, and as you pray, you get an idea on how to save money by substituting those white orchids with white roses. With this whole wedding process, one thing is guaranteed: if you ask Him for help or advice, He will give it to you…if you have ears to hear.

Father, *I want to sit at Your table today and just talk with You. I have so many concerns about this wedding, and I want to hear what You have to say about them. I'm open to any ideas, suggestions, and thoughts You might have, because I know You always have my best interest at heart. You called me because You love me, and for that, I am so very grateful. Talking with You calms my spirit and puts everything right once again in my life. Thank You.*

THOUGHTS OF GOD'S GOODNESS

DAY 19

Making a Space for Him

Move over and give him some closet space in your heart.

But thou, when thou prayest, enter into thy closet, and when thou hast shut thy door, pray to thy Father which is in secret; and thy Father which seeth in secret shall reward thee openly.

—Matthew 6:6

Now we need to discuss that hallowed place that every woman has—her closet. You know what I am talking about. When you were a child, did you ever have to share a closet with your siblings? Maybe at college you had to split a closet with four roommates. Will you ever forget jamming all those jeans, shorts, tops, skirts, dress pants, shoes, and purses into that wee space? Your tops looked like accordion fans, and your long pants were crinkled into capris way before they were in style.

Then that momentous event occurred: you moved out and finally had an entire closet all to yourself. Those lined-up shoes would make the clerks at Macy's salivate. And how about those outfits? All color coordinated, are they?

Let's liken your various closets with your heart. When you were young, you had a lot of relationships jammed into your heart; your family, friends, and relatives. Finally the day came

when you moved into your own place, and your heart was opened only to those you chose to share it with.

Well it's time again to move your stuff over and allow someone else into your space. After having all that freedom, you are once again going to have to share some of your space. It's time to get rid of a lot of old stuff—things you don't really need anymore—because you have to make some space for the man you love. Remember how frustrated you were with that mini locker space? Well, so will your mate be, if you don't give him some room in your heart.

You're not going to lose your entire heart; you're just going to make some adjustments, like throwing out unnecessary and outdated items so there's plenty of room for him to move in. He is going to bring some questionable things into your relationship too, so don't get aggravated with him. Today you may be sharing a tiny space in your heart, but if you allow him in, you will be talking about a huge walk-in closet you both share someday. And if you are real nice, he might even let you color coordinate his T-shirts!

Father, *teach me to trust this man I love. Show me the mystery of opening up my heart to another. I don't want past hurts or bad relationships to deter me from giving all I can to this marriage. Give me the innocence of a child, the ability to see through eyes devoid of fear, and the grace to make this man welcome in my heart.*

Thoughts of Making My Mate Welcome

DAY 20

SWEET HOLIDAYS WITH THE FAMILIES

Or is it the Great Divide?

And the king said, Divide the living child in two, and give half to the one, and half to the other. Then spake the woman whose the living child was unto the king, for her bowels yearned upon her son, and she said, O my lord, give her the living child, and in no wise slay it. But the other said, Let it be neither mine nor thine, but divide it. Then the king answered…, Give her the living child, and in no wise slay it: she is the mother thereof.

—1 Kings 3:25–27

Adding to the stress of your wedding plans, you may encounter some other problems if your engagement runs through any holidays. You have never had to make decisions as to where you would spend your holidays; you just knew where you would be. Now you have to maneuver through them as if land mines were planted all around you. You must step very carefully, because all along the way, you might find little bombs with hair-trigger fuses. All it takes to detonate one is to disregard a family tradition, not recognize "it is always done this way," or suggest a new sweet potato casserole instead of the time-honored sweet potatoes coated with burnt marshmallows.

These dilemmas will have you feeling like the wishbone on that fat, golden-basted turkey. When you begin to feel pulled in too many directions, get with your mate so the two of you can establish some guidelines. Sometimes, a situation arises for which no absolutely happy solution can be found; this is when

you need to determine what works best for the two of you, and go with it.

Here's the upside to this. Isn't it grand that everyone is clamoring for your company? You can have the best of both worlds. Seek the wisdom of the Lord, have a gracious heart, and be willing to share. Now your mom and dad, siblings, and Auntie Mabel are all going to have to make some adjustments, so go easy on them. They have always been used to you being there to help decorate the tree, chop celery for the Thanksgiving dressing, and make the hard-boiled eggs for Easter, but we all have to adapt in life. Remember, you are not the only one who is going through some tremendous changes.

There are many ways to resolve the holiday situations; the secret is to make sure no one feels forgotten or left out—and that includes you and your mate. As you create a life together, you will eventually want to make traditions for your own family to carry on. Holidays involve spending time with family, sharing special moments, and reestablishing the importance of being a family. When you start to feel that tugging, just realize you are experiencing it only because everyone wants to spend time with you, and for that, you are blessed.

Father, *I thank You for family. Help me to make wise decisions, and give me the wisdom of Solomon through these holidays. Please bless my new family, and show me how to embrace this brand-new family as a gift from You.*

SPECIAL HOLIDAY THOUGHTS

21 · DAY ·

YOUR CHILDHOOD

Don't expend energy on things you can't change.

Brethren, I count not myself to have apprehended:
but this one thing I do, forgetting those things which are behind,
and reaching forth unto those things which are before,
I press toward the mark for the prize of the
high calling of God in Christ Jesus.
—Philippians 3:13–15

Teddy bears slump dejectedly on their shelves. Garbage bags are packed with all your childhood memories: tattered pom-poms, battered tennis rackets, and treasure boxes filled with valentines from first grade. The walls look like a patchwork quilt, with empty spaces where your friend's smiling faces used to peek out from their dusty picture frames. You are packing up. It's time to leave your childhood home.

Do you feel the stillness around you? Your family doesn't quite know how to handle this. They sense their upcoming loss: one less person at the dinner table, your laughter no longer drifting through the house, and your absence. We all fear the unknown, and dramatic changes can be quite unsettling, so it is normal to feel a bit apprehensive. It's similar to a time of mourning, yet a time of great rejoicing, too. Your family may feel like they are losing someone they love. A thousand memories are pulling you back in time, but your heart is pushing you forward.

Your childhood will never be left behind; it lies nestled in the memories you hold dear. Those memories are not tangible items that can be brushed away by freshly painted walls, a cleaned-out closet, or your mom's exercise equipment in your old room. You may be leaving your childlike ways behind, but God has so many wonderful new experiences awaiting you! You won't believe me right now, but I'm telling you, six months from now, that old baby doll with the one good eye and the chopped off hair, which you hold so dear today, will be relegated to a cardboard box in the garage. In fact, she will probably be packed into the carton your deluxe mixer wedding present came in.

You are not forgetting about these special items; you are just setting them aside. In years to come, you will stumble over that dented cardboard box, open it, and cradle your baby doll once again. As you sit huddled in the cold garage, warm memories will wash over you…and then you will hear your husband call you. Pop! Back she goes, into her box, until she is again rediscovered and warms your heart another day.

Father, *help me take the good memories with me, and give me the courage to leave the bad ones behind. Thank You for always understanding me. Please make me aware of what the people I love are experiencing, and show me their needs as I pack up my childhood. Give me vision for the future You have in store for me.*

WEEK FOUR

• *Wedding Tips* •

Checklist: Finalize your guest list. Book a makeup artist and hairstylist. Order your wedding favors. Shop for candles, ring pillow, items for gift bags, guest bathroom froufrou (lotions, mints, etc.), guest book, and pen. Gather special photos you want to have displayed.

• • •

To make a special moment at your reception, consider doing this: Provide a white candle to each of your guests. Relight your unity candle, and start a chain of lights with all your guests. Dance your first dance in the romantic candlelight provided by your friends and family.

· DAY 22 ·

DON'T TAKE THINGS SO SERIOUSLY

It will cause wrinkles.

Therefore I say unto you, take no thought for your life, what ye shall eat, or what ye shall drink; nor yet for your body, what ye shall put on. Is not the life more than meat, and the body than raiment?

—Matthew 6:25

The most memorable moments of weddings are the hilarious mishaps that occur. No matter what happens, you must believe God is in control. That doesn't mean things won't go wrong; it means He will be there to make whatever occurs all right.

The florist might deliver the flowers late, and your ring bearer may troop down the aisle in full tux and sneakers. But that's life, and life happens. If you go with the flow and don't fight it, you will find hidden delights in what the world terms *mistakes*. In reality, you are dealing with thousands of details, so you must build in a margin of error. Anyone who works with numbers or formulas will tell you that they always create a reservoir in the equation to allow for a small amount of miscalculation.

Worry and anxiety will burn your fuel, and when you permit them to creep in, you'll find your energy draining out as fast as handbags fly off the shelves at a buy one, get one free sale. To

conserve your energy, don't dwell on the what-ifs or on things you don't have the power to change. The Word tells us to press toward the mark, so keep going forward.

Your wedding day holds a lot of unknowns, but I can give you one guarantee that will bring you some comfort: I guarantee that no matter what happens, the Lord will be with you and will make this day one you will remember all your life. At one of the weddings Jesus personally attended, the host ran out of wine, and Jesus helped them out of that faux pas. Relax. He knows how to make things happen—how to make things right.

Over the coming days, one positive thing you can do is to develop a comfort phrase or slogan you can repeat when things don't go exactly as you planned. This slogan will give you the ability to laugh at the circumstances, which will immediately diminish their importance. My pet phrase is this: "Whatever it takes." If you run into a roadblock or mountain, "whatever it takes" to get around or over it—that is what you need to do. So quit frowning, and put a smile on your face. Remember, you're getting married!

Father, *thank You for giving me a "whatever it takes" attitude. With that gift, I can have faith to speak to mountains and pull down walls that would try to hem me in. I know that if I keep my eyes on You, whatever we do together will be a success. Be with your people who have huge problems, and I ask You to answer their pleas for help.*

DAY 23

Believe What He Tells You!

Even if you don't want to hear it, believe it.

For he that will love life, and see good days,
let him refrain his tongue from evil,
and his lips that they speak no guile.
—1 Peter 3:10

You are well into the wedding process by now, and I'm sure you've had some encounters with your intended, as far as wedding details go. You have a Cinderella vision of the whole day, and all he sees is one big party. Have you asked his opinion on anything yet: the flowers, the cake, or the reception hall? Most men are not really into the cute little details, but some do want to be involved in what's going on. He might have just a wee part in the entire ordeal, but give him the respect of acknowledging what he does want. Yes, even if he wants the groom's cake to be an exact replica of his fraternity's mascot, the opossum.

If you ask him a question or want his opinion, believe what he tells you. The people who are close to you will probably speak what they feel. You might be tempted to ignore their statements, and this is where trouble can occur. Here's an example: Your maid of honor shows up to take you to lunch and tells you she is

in a bad mood. Subconsciously, she just forewarned you. But hey, you think, nah, she's always joking. You continue through lunch and run on and on about every little wedding detail. Suddenly she snaps at you. This shocks you, because she is always Little Miss Sunshine. I mean, after all, what could possibly be upsetting her? She doesn't have a wedding to plan. Now you are hurt and feel betrayed. You rely on her sunny attitude, and here she is blowing a gasket. Think back. She forewarned you. She plainly told you she was in a bad mood, so you have no right to be upset with her. Instead of going on and on about the wedding, maybe you should have spent some time listening to her needs.

If your intended shows up for date night looking tired, and he says he's ready to explode after the day he's had, believe what he says, and watch out. He has told you in so many words that he's looking for an avenue to let off that bomb. Don't handle that TNT and think you can escape the incinerating blast that's going to come. Now, if you want to try and defuse the bomb, that's a different story. Using tact, understanding, and wisdom, you might end up with a wonderful evening together. This is when he needs you to hear what he is saying, so cock that pretty head, close those sweet lips, and open those ears. Ahhh, mission accomplished!

Father, *I thank You that the Word holds so much wisdom. I'm going to need some help with this issue. Help me control my tongue, hear with my heart, and believe what those I love are telling me. Make me sensitive to the needs of others, and give me the gift of timing that I may know when to back off and when to move in.*

THOUGHTS OF WORDS HE'S SAID

DAY 24

A Multitude of Counsel

Are too many chiefs involved?

"Now listen to me: I will give you counsel, and God be with you. You be the people's representative before God, and you bring the disputes to God."

—Exodus 18:19 (NASB)

In life, everyone wants to be the quarterback, the leader, the director, or the manager. It's human nature for us to want to control situations. This is a wedding, not a full-scale Broadway production, so you do not need to have a wardrobe coordinator, a choreographer, and a personal assistant. A multitude of counsel may offer safety, but that counsel is only helpful if you are unsure of what you want.

In this production, only one director is needed—you. You've got the script already written, you know the cast you want, and you've already set the stage for the final scene where the guy on the white horse rides into the sunset with the girl, and that, too, is you. Too many opinions only bring confusion. At times, you may need advice; that's what your professionals—your florist, cake decorator, wedding planner, and such—are for.

If you listen to everyone, you will discover yourself getting further and further away from what you initially wanted. You'll

wake up one morning and find yourself tiptoeing down the aisle in a pencil thin gown instead of floating down the aisle in your princess wedding dress. At your reception, you'll be dancing the polka instead of hooting and line dancing. You'll be staring at dried fruit table ornaments versus sparkling, fairy-lit candles. Things can turn bad very quickly.

How do you graciously maintain control without hurting anyone's feelings? You do it through prayer, continual centering of yourself, and a sharp focus on the ultimate goal—your wedding day. You pat many hands, give lots of hugs, offer honest thank-yous, and administer a whole bunch of "I'll pray on that's" to suggestions given. It is important to remember everyone means well and wants this day to be special for you.

Father, *thank You for all the loving support that surrounds me. I'm so happy to finally be planning my wedding, and I'm grateful for all You have provided me. If I make some errors, let those You have around me lift me up and provide me with prayerful support. I welcome the wisdom of those I love.*

Thoughts of Counsel I Need

25 DAY

YOUR DEMEANOR DICTATES YOUR DAY

Keep smiling.

I call heaven and earth to record this day against you, that I have set before you life and death, blessing and cursing: therefore choose life, that both thou and thy seed may live.

—Deuteronomy 30:19

The Lord has granted you a wonderful gift called *choice*, and He specifically says to choose life. Today you have the opportunity to direct the path your life will take. Your tire has gone flat, your nail broke, and you've misplaced the photographer's phone number, so you have an immediate choice to make. You can kick the car, snag your hose with your jagged nail, and scream at your mom to help you find the photographer's number, or you can stop and recognize that, somehow, you are totally out of the flow of life.

Instead of wading through the backwash, take a moment to settle down, seek the Lord, and make a conscious decision not to get upset. Begin to praise the Lord, and you will see things turn around. Put a smile on your face, and don't allow the enemy to steal your joy. This is how you get victory. You'll be surprised how powerful you will feel. Why? Because focusing on God puts you in the flow of life again.

When you practice this, you will have the ability to spread the good news, change someone's life, make a difference. If you want blessings to flow toward you, give some out. It might take only a smile to divert the depression that's overtaking your co-worker. Tell the store clerk how beautiful her complexion is, or help an elderly woman by holding the door open for her while giving her one of your dazzling smiles.

When your mate asks how your day is going, you may tell him about the problems you had, but then be sure to tell him how you turned your day around. This kind of attitude is contagious. Next time he is faced with an unpleasant situation, he will remember how you took control of your day and directed it toward life and blessings. You're the kind of woman he is looking for, one who smiles in the face of disaster, rises above unpleasant situations, and keeps on going.

Father, *today I choose life and blessings, not curses. Help me overcome obstacles with a smile on my face, and use me as an instrument of Your peace to bring joy and hope to those who cross my path. Let me look back with honor at the stressful days before my wedding, satisfied that I stayed the course, kept smiling, and blessed others along the way. Please bring joy to those who are sad and lonely today.*

· DAY ·

TIME TOGETHER

Set that wedding planner aside.

And Jacob served seven years for Rachel; and they seemed unto him but a few days, for the love he had to her.

—Genesis 29:20

Time is a definitive gift that can't be returned, refunded, or rebated. As you can see from the above Scripture, Jacob worked seven years just so he could be near the love of his life, Rachel. He labored in the hot sun day after day, watching the one he loved; yet he was unable to claim her as his own. Time spent in her presence was enough for him. Now that is love!

Don't take your mate for granted. Today is a good day to let him know that, amidst all the wedding turmoil, he still takes center stage. Be spontaneous. Why don't you give him a call and plan a quiet lunch or dinner together—and no wedding talk allowed. I know it's hard to find time, but if you can't spare two or three hours out of your schedule, then something is amiss to begin with. After all, who's in control here?

Let the wedding storm rage all around you, but resist the winds of that twister that is trying to suck you into its vortex. A place of escape from all your anxiety can be found in the

company of the one you love. When the winds blow, hold on to each other, and wait for the storm to pass. Subdued lighting, quiet music, and the gentle sound of voices filtering through the restaurant will calm you down, and the only wind you will feel will be the gentle breeze created by the whirling fans overhead. Shhhhhhhhhh.

Reminisce together about what brought you to this point in your lives. You might want to let him know how good he looked in those jeans; maybe it was the quirky smile he gave you or the way your eyes met across a crowded room that drew the two of you together. Go back and keep going back to those days when the earth stood still and you felt you couldn't make it through the day if you didn't hear his voice or feel his touch.

These suggestions might sound silly, but what could be more important than being together? The precious gift of time is seldom valued until it is gone. There are no guaranteed tomorrows, no assurances of buttery sunrises or violet sunsets. The only time you know you have is now, this moment, so live it to the fullest. Come on, this is not a monumental task; it's a wonderful lunch or dinner we're talking about. Have some *fun*!

Father, *please give me an awareness of time. Let me always view time with my love as a gift, and let me never be nonchalant about life and its value. Help me put aside wedding thoughts, and show me how to let my love know how much I value his friendship and company. And Father, thank You for having time for me today.*

THOUGHTS OF PRIORITIES

DAY 27

WORKING AS A TEAM

You gotta let him play.

We then, as workers together with him, beseech you also that ye receive not the grace of God in vain.

—2 Corinthians 6:1

That privately owned business called Your Life is about to undergo a major corporate restructuring. When you became engaged, you entered into a merger, an agreement that two individuals would combine everything they have and form a new company. As with all mergers, many changes are going to be taking place, and unfortunately, they won't all be in your favor.

We are talking about two merging into one to create a better, stronger, and more fulfilling life for both of you. This is a joint partnership, so both interests must be encouraged to express their ideas and visions. You are no longer a single entity making all the decisions, calling all the shots, and receiving all the rewards. You and your mate are investing the same amount into this venture: each of you is bringing your life to the table. This is a very costly enterprise, so no one wants to be slighted, and the way to ensure both of you get a fair share is encouraging equal participation.

You might not like some of the decisions or changes he makes, but unbeknownst to you, he might not be too happy with some of the changes you are making either. Here's where that "ouch" word, *compromise*, comes in. I know that word hurts, and you never had to use it when you were single, but in the corporate world of marriage you are now entering, it will become your company motto. The good news is that many perks come with this. You will have a new name, great family benefits, and a stronger financial core, and this is one instance in which a sexual relationship on the job is welcomed.

We are not talking about a corporate takeover here; we are talking about taking two winners and combining their humor, spirit, and gifts to form a union that will be unstoppable. The surprise is how much richer your life can be when it is undergirded with the strengths of your mate. With the Lord as your CEO, there's no way you can fail. And what a pension plan you are investing into! This one pays daily dividends of smiles, hugs, love, and trust. The Fortune 500 Club can take a hike; this company's listed in the Lamb's Book of Life!

Father, *teach me how to play in this game called life, and show me how to adapt to the changes that are coming my way. I know my mate was raised under Your hand, so let me not slight him or diminish his personal dreams. Help me to walk hand in hand with my partner, and please give us Your blessing in this union.*

THOUGHTS OF THE BENEFITS OF MERGING

DAY 28

Anger Management 101

Attendance is required.

He that is slow to anger is better than the mighty; and he that ruleth his spirit than he that taketh a city.

—Proverbs 16:32

Anger is usually the result of frustration because you cannot control a situation. Think about it. You have just learned that you are going to be charged extra for alterations on your wedding gown, and you are foaming at the mouth. Tons of arguments run through your mind as to why you should not be charged, but you are cornered. The frustration sometimes mounts to seething rage in these situations. What can you do?

Well, what price are you willing to pay for the wedding dress you have always dreamed of wearing? If, in your heart, you know you would have paid whatever it cost at the time you saw it, then calm down, put a smile on your face, and shell out the money.

It is OK to be mad every once in a while. Your expectations of people don't always come through: some people don't operate on the same level of integrity as you do, and a few just plain don't have a conscience. In other words, you are all playing the game, but not everyone plays by the same rules. How do you get past

this? Why not go blow off some steam today at the gym or the sauna? Don't let yourself get bitter over things that are not in your control. Let it go, as hard as that might be. What do you hope to gain by being angry? Does it help to have a slobbering pity party because things have not gone your way? Well, maybe. If it does, do it, and get over it.

You may also experience episodes of anger in your relationship with your intended. That is OK, because anger can be very constructive: it motivates change and gets things out in the open where they can be dealt with. So if you get angry with your mate, air your differences, but then pour on the balm. You may pout for a short while, and a little door slamming may be OK as long as you don't jolt the pictures off the walls. But whenever you experience confrontation or conflict in your relationship with your mate, you *must* work to make things right.

Harboring anger and resentment is absolute poison to your system, so get rid of it as quickly as you can. It can also put a damper on your relationship with the Lord. So deal with anger as best you can, put it behind you, and pour your energy into things you can control.

Father, *thank You for anger and the improvements it can bring about. I recognize it as a tool to release the pressure inside me. When I get so steamed up inside, it's good to know You have a release valve that I can open to let out all this hot air before I explode. Teach me how to express my anger without sinning.* If I have burned anyone through angry words or actions, teach me how to apply the balm of Gilead to heal the relationship.*

*See Ephesians 4:26.

Thoughts of Anger I Want to Dispel

WEEK FIVE

• *Wedding Tips* •

Checklist: Mail your wedding invitations. Finalize the rehearsal dinner plans. Write your vows. Check your registry, and update your wedding Web site. Purchase gifts for parents and attendants. Shop for bridal accessories, such as garter, jewelry, and purse. Check with your mom and mother-in-law about their wardrobes.

• • •

Every contract should cover basic points, and most contain the phrase "time is of the essence," meaning the date of the contracted service is an essential part of the agreement. Pay with a credit card to protect against a company's no-show, demise, or unscrupulous behavior. You will have a better chance of repayment if your credit card company disputes the charges.

BUT IT'S YOUR WEDDING!

Who cares what Auntie Mabel wants?

Wherefore take unto you the whole armour of God, that ye may be able to withstand in the evil day, and having done all, to stand. Stand therefore, having your loins girt about with truth, and having on the breastplate of righteousness; and your feet shod with the preparation of the gospel of peace; above all, taking the shield of faith, wherewith ye shall be able to quench all the fiery darts of the wicked. And take the helmet of salvation, and the sword of the Spirit, which is the word of God.

—Ephesians 6:13–17

Your quaint chapel wedding has bloomed into a cathedral fiasco, your tasty buffet has swelled into a seven-course dinner, and your four intimate attendants have ballooned into a family reunion at the altar. The agenda has evolved into a queen's coronation, with the Beverly Hillbillies coordinating it. How did your fantasy wedding turn into a full-blown Broadway production? Yikes! What to do, what to do?

Stop it. It's that simple. Now is the time to dig your jeweled stilettos into the ground, firmly place your veiled tiara onto your head, put up your saucy shield of faith, and stand. Ever since you were little, you have envisioned your perfect wedding, and now you are about to give birth to that dream. This is what you are fighting for.

When you are confronted with a million suggestions from every relative who is a self-proclaimed wedding expert, keep this

thought paramount in your mind: *Auntie Mabel and all the others have already had their day.* It's your turn, and it's important that you don't feel obligated to do what others want. Who's the bride here? Once you take a stand for what you want, confusion will dissipate and order will be reestablished. People really do want to help, and that is exactly what they are there for—to help and execute the bride's wishes.

Everyone will be taking their cues from you, so if you appear in control, they will relax. Remember, you can shut down this production anytime you want. For a wedding, all you really need are the blessing of the Lord, your mate, and the person the Lord would have marry you. See, you're good to go. I told you it was that simple! Today, relax in the knowledge that even if some of your peripheral plans were to go awry, you could still accomplish your main objective, which is to marry the one you love.

Father, *today I seek Your unmerited favor upon these wedding plans. I ask for Your wisdom and Your miraculous sense of divine order to operate in my life. Give me words as sweet as honey to pour upon others who may easily get their feelings hurt and the courage to stand up and fight for my dream with no guilt or condemnation.*

DAY 30

YOU'RE LOSING IT

It's meltdown time.

I am weary of my crying: my throat is dried:
mine eyes fail while I wait for my God.
—Psalm 69:3

You've got two more months to go, and everything seems to be unraveling. The invitations are delayed, your mom can't find a dress, and one of your bridesmaids dropped 20 pounds after being fitted for her gown! Take a deep breath and remember who is in charge of this wedding. You gave this affair to the Lord, right?

Your emotions are springing up and plunging down like a free-falling bungee jumper. It is OK to cry. Think of your body as a battery-charged device and your meltdown may make a little more sense. When you first buy a cell phone or anything that requires batteries, the instructions usually say to let the battery run all the way down. Then when you charge it up, it gets a good, strong, full charge. When your body is wearing down bit by bit, you don't realize it until there is just nothing left to draw from. When you get to that point, just sit down and have a good cry. And yes, you may also get out that pint of ice cream. When you

do this, you empty yourself of all the negative, murky emotions that are clouding up your soul.

Let the worries and frustrations pour out of you. Curl up in bed, cry your eyes out, put on an old movie, and pamper yourself by allowing the meltdown to happen gently and privately. Tomorrow is another day, but today, go with the flow of your emotions, and let them take you wherever they want to go. You have been constraining yourself and doing a very good job, so luxuriate in your woe. It is not going to become a lifestyle for you, so don't be afraid of it.

We have been taught that to cry or to lose control is a sign of weakness. Yet I have experienced the greatest presence of the Lord when I was at my weakest. Let Him have control, because He knows exactly what He is doing.

When you are totally drained, you will feel a nothingness, an "I don't care about anything" attitude. This is good. You are not allowing problems to have power over you. You are now ready to be plugged in and recharged. This is when you will see the tremendous power of God. He will bring a renewing, a refreshing to your spirit and soul. When you are weak, then He is strong (see 2 Corinthians 12:9). Are you ready to see the miraculous power of God? Let the boo-hoos begin!

Father, *I've had it. I don't think I can go on for one more moment. My thoughts are reeling, everything is out of whack, and I'm absolutely exhausted. For just a while, I am going to lay my head upon Your lap and cry my eyes out. Tomorrow is another day.*

31 · DAY ·

He's Driving You Crazy

He doesn't get it.

And I have filled him with the spirit of God, in wisdom, and in understanding, and in knowledge, and in all manner of workmanship.

—Exodus 31:3

Oh my, did you see that china pattern he said he liked? Does he really think every time you sit down to eat you want to look at that gosh awful horseshoe pattern splashed around the rim of those turquoise plates? What could he have been thinking about? Urg! Who is this man anyway?

And another thing, how can he be so happy-go-lucky, when you are so burdened with all the wedding details? You just want to bite his head off. Doesn't he understand how important it is to get those invitations stuffed just so and how vital it is to have postage stamps that match the motif on the invitation? And he wonders why you are spiraling out of control. Does he realize you can't just plop ten more guests onto the guest list? And how about the honeymoon? He has some crazy notion that you would love to hike the Oregon Trail armed with 40 pounds of hardware strapped to your back and lathered in bug spray instead of that luscious vanilla body cream you bought with hopes of enticing him.

The list goes on and on, and it looks like you are headed for the definitive showdown where you will speak those infamous words, "You just don't understand me."

No he doesn't understand. You have dreamt of your wedding since the first time you dressed your doll in that stiff, jeweled wedding dress and placed the tiara on her golden ringlets. As long as you can remember, you've been subconsciously moving toward your amble down the aisle. He, on the other hand, has been running around bases and jogging through life. He's not been on the journey you have. All he sees is the prize at the finish line—and it's you. He doesn't care how he gets there or who's cheering him on along the way.

So while you are navigating your way toward the goal, stopping to pluck a daisy here and admiring a butterfly there, he is whizzing past you, sweat and all, to the finish line. See, he does get it after all; maybe you're the one who has lost your way.

Father, *so many women are still searching for the man of their dreams, and I pray they find him. I am blessed beyond measure to have this wonderful guy. He's one of a kind, and I thank You for his uniqueness.*

DAY 32

Lord, Did I Make a Mistake?

Does every bride feel like this?

Teach me, and I will hold my tongue:
and cause me to understand wherein I have erred.
—Job 6:24

Did I make a mistake? This is a question every bride asks—and rightly so. We should always be open to hear the voice of the Lord, and as the Scripture says, He will teach us and cause us to understand. But if you have not had any hesitation in your heart, then you are probably just experiencing wedding jitters. Right now you are going through tremendous changes, and the future is full of uncertainty.

The old adage, the grass is always greener on the other side, can wreak havoc in your mind. Some of the thoughts that drive you crazy are, "Maybe there is someone better out there," "What if he changes?" or "He might not be everything I want him to be." Life has no guarantees, but if you have sought the blessing of the Lord, and He appears to approve of your choice, why, that's the gold seal of approval.

Because you both are smack-dab in the middle of this huge wedding project, you are experiencing some emotions and seeing

some sides of each other that you have never felt or seen before. Look at this positively: you have a bird's-eye view of how you both react under pressure, and, hopefully, you are pulling together to get through this mess.

So how do you get assurance that you made the right choice? As always, you turn your face toward God and pray. He will calm the storm within you. Take some time to walk in the cool of the evening with Him, as Adam did. Because you have His friendship, you don't have to be like other brides who are weighed down with apprehension and worry. You can go to Him, and with a word, He will still your mind, erase your doubts, and cause you to see the wise decision you have made.

You are looking at the mere outline of a book entitled, *Your Life,* but don't forget that Jesus is the author and finisher of your faith. *Your Life*, when written by His hand, will be well crafted, and if it is anything like His last best-seller, the Bible, then I guarantee you, it will have a happy ending.

Father, *I thank You for guidance. I ask You to bless all those who are involved with my wedding. So many are giving of their time, and I am so grateful for that. I pray happiness for those who are in need of some joy and love for those who are lonely.*

THOUGHTS ON WHY I CHOOSE THIS MAN

DAY 33

MIND GAMES

Set up a firewall.

Thou wilt keep him in perfect peace, whose mind is stayed on thee: because he trusteth in thee.

—Isaiah 26:3

Thoughts are pummeling your mind. If your mom questions you one more time about the vows you've planned or if Grandma Bea asks again if she's going to get a corsage, you may scream. When problems and questions come in rapid succession, it is difficult to keep your calm demeanor. They are as irritating as those pop-ups on your computer and just as difficult to eradicate. How can you politely tell everyone to take a hike?

If you don't get control of the situation, your mind will follow the direction of the voice that speaks the loudest. Your visions and ideas will weaken and meekly begin to reflect the voice blasting out of the bullhorn. You know if you get three people together, they won't all come to the same conclusion, because everyone sees things from a different perspective. So to avoid mass chaos, don't ask for opinions unless you really need them.

The Bible tells us to guard our minds, so there must be a reason for it. Our minds can become prey to things that will

ultimately try to do us in. It is very difficult to get your mind under control when you have ten chattering voices wooing you this way or that. Don't you sometimes want to clamp your hands over your ears and tell everyone to be quiet? When you reach this point, your body is telling you it has had enough.

Jesus often left the group He was with to go off and pray. He needed to get away from the crowd of voices, and so do you. It takes time to sort through the barrage of voices in your mind, to decipher which ones are valid and instructional and which ones are meant to hurt and destroy you. And yes, unfortunately, there are some who would like to see you fall flat on your pretty face as you regally stroll down the aisle.

Time spent in solitude clears your mind. Like a soldier in training, you must start disciplining your mind to go where you tell it, calm down when you instruct it to, and be on alert when you prod it. You must constantly war to control your thoughts. Under that filmy veil, you had better be packing your sword, the Word of God, covertly hidden in the recesses of your mind. Are you prepared with prayer, the Word, and God's promises? Then let the games begin!

Father, *give me a warrior mentality, and awaken me from this slumber I have been in. Keep me alert, on guard, and ready at all times to use the weapons You have given me for protection and power in my life. As for warfare strategy, I might need more of Your help with that one. I pray comfort for those who are separated from their loved ones, whether it be through war, sickness, or death.*

THOUGHTS OF GOD'S PROTECTION

DAY 34

IS THIS LOVE REAL?

Or have you gotten a cheap imitation?

This Mary, whose brother Lazarus now lay sick, was the same one who poured perfume on the Lord and wiped his feet with her hair.

—John 11:2 (NIV)

Tons of mayonnaise can disguise imitation lobster, and a knockoff purse can be passed off as an original as long as no one looks too close. For some things in life, you can skate through with facsimiles because you are not looking for craftsmanship or quality; you just want to convey an image. Love is one area in which you cannot afford to settle for less than the real thing, because though it appears you are saving something, it will cost you dearly in the long run.

Some of your previous partners may have been good-lookers, fantastic flatterers, wooing cavaliers, or charming gents, but something was missing in all of them, which is why you did not marry them. They may not have all been imitations, but they were missing some vital characteristics you were searching for. When you clink pure crystal, it emits a beautiful, perfectly pitched sound. When you jangled certain nerves in your prior relationships, you subconsciously heard a dull thud.

So what is it you were looking for, and how can you tell if your intended is the genuine real thing? After all, love is not a tangible thing that can be measured or contained. I classify love into two types: "pretty love" and "raw love." Pretty love is the outer layer: flowers, music, stardust, and shimmering dreams. Then there is raw love, which is the real thing. It's there when you're sick, when you haven't a penny to share, when discouragement shrouds your vision and you feel there is no hope of ever climbing out of the pit you're in. Raw love softly strokes your hair back from your sweaty brow, splits a can of soup with you (giving you all the noodles), and reaches for your hand to pull you out of that pit.

Pretty love has no strength within itself, but raw love is powerful. Raw love is naked emotions played out across the kitchen table. If you are wondering whether you have the real thing or not, size up your mate. Has he shown himself strong in times of conflict? If so, then he is made of quality. Does he have lasting abilities? Then he has endurance. Does he make you feel safe? Then he is a mountain of a man. If you answered yes to these questions, then praise the Lord! It sounds like you've got yourself some raw love, and you only have to look around to know that's a rare commodity these days.

Father, *thank You for creating love. How bland life would be without this wonderful emotion! Help me honor this man and see him for all he is in Your eyes. I'm thankful You thought enough of me to send him into my life. I will love him, always.*

THOUGHTS OF LOVE'S MANY FACES

35 · DAY ·

HIGH-HEELED EXPECTATIONS

Are your expectations too high, guaranteeing a fall?

And now, Lord, what wait I for?
My hope is in thee.
—Psalm 39:7

Do you ever feel great anticipation before going to a movie that everyone raves about? By the time you get to see it, your imagination blows it up to be a cinematic masterpiece. Let's face it, during the scene in the pet shop where Katie finds the puppy she has always wanted, unless that pup romps out of the screen and licks your face, the movie just doesn't measure up to your expectations.

How about when you see those supercool shoes? That three-inch heel is for the experienced only, but the tweed pattern is just so darling and would perfectly match your fringed bolero jacket. So what do you do? You risk life and limb, climb onto those fashion statements, and precariously walk down the store aisle. You hold on to the shelves for support, because they are the only things separating you from sheer disaster. Is the pain really worth it? Wouldn't you feel more comfortable in those one-inch slingbacks?

The same could be said for your wedding. I know you have visions of doves taking flight in numbered succession and butterflies fluttering out of their captivity at the count of five. Unfortunately, not all of the million tiny details of your wedding can be so controlled. If you allow for some minor mishaps, some not-so-perfect moments, then you will be so much more comfortable. Walking precariously through your wedding planning can take the joy out of these special moments for you. Sometimes it's refreshing to throw on some old sneakers and run through the whole process.

As you go jogging through the details, you can brush off those words of warning about that carrot cake being so heavy it may topple over. So what? If it topples, then you will deal with it. How about the warnings that it may rain? Keep running. You can always seat those guests in the reception hall and make your grand entrance through the double doors. As long as you are willing to be flexible and have alternative plans, dump those constraining heels and run like the wind! See, there *is* life during your engagement!

Father, *please give me the ability to adapt to any circumstances I may encounter in life. Help me to have an attitude that nothing is impossible when I have You in my life. Make me an overcomer in all of life's situations. And I pray for those who have lost the strength to run. Help them to walk and not be weary, to run and not faint, and to rise up with wings as eagles.**

*See Isaiah 40:31.

THOUGHTS OF MY EXPECTATIONS

Week Six

• *Wedding Tips* •

Checklist: Set up a filing system for RSVPs, and check on hotel reservations for your guests. Meet with the photographer, and outline what pictures you definitely want taken. Shop for table decorations and end of the evening items, such as sparklers and bubbles.

• • •

On your wedding program, list each person in the wedding party, their relationship to you and your intended, and a fun tidbit as to why they are special to you.

DAY 36

Where Did Your Mom Go?

She's not hearing you.

Honour thy father and thy mother: that thy days may be long upon the land which the LORD thy God giveth thee.

—Exodus 20:12

Did you honestly think you would get through this whole devotional without the above Scripture? Yes, this is something the Lord would like for you to do. And no, you cannot keep having that vision of your mother silently being strangled by the automatic seat belt. Not all mothers behave ideally when their daughters get married, but the majority of them do want only the best for their daughters. You have no idea the number of hours your mom has spent on her knees petitioning the Lord for a mate for you. See, she does have a stake in all of this, too.

Your mom is dealing with her own issues as you get married. She may be wondering how or where she fits into your new world. She is having to take two steps back and watch as you begin your separation from her, and this can be a floundering experience for her. Suddenly the time you spend together, the intimate phone calls, and the lazy shopping days are threatened. She now has

an alien, soon to be called son-in-law, contending for your time and affections.

She is experiencing the empty nest syndrome all over again, even though you may have been out of the house for years. It's the whole concept that scares her. She's not familiar with this strange woman she's riding in the car with as you two go to pick out bridal flowers. Where did this self-confident, focused woman come from? Your mom still sees the shy little girl who ran back to give her a hug on the first day of school. She doesn't see you in that dazzling wedding dress; she sees you in your ballerina tutu twirling, you in puffed sleeves for your sixth grade dance, and you dressed as an angel for the Christmas school play.

Mom is having a rough time right now, and this is where you can really make a difference. Take the time to talk to her. Give her some assurance of how important she is to you, and let her know that will never change. Thank her for always being there for you, and I promise you, she will hear every word you say. Now, pick up that ringing phone and answer it. Yep, it's your mom again. Never forget, she's still the greatest at making chocolate chip cookies, and she's never too busy for you.

Father, *thank You for moms. Help me to be patient and see through the eyes of my mother. Make me sensitive to her needs, and let me never disregard all the things she has done for me over the years. Help me to show her patience and love during this time.*

Grateful Thoughts of My Mother

DAY 37

DAD HAS DESERTED YOU

Why is he so distant?

Now the LORD had said unto Abram, Get thee out of thy country, and from thy kindred, and from thy father's house, unto a land that I will shew thee.

—Genesis 12:1

Dad has not deserted you; he's just lost in a forest, separated from you by a chasm called "womanhood." Ever since you were born, he has been your knight, battling for you, his princess. He has scoured the countryside to fulfill your needs, hid among the trees to catch marauding jackals who tried to steal your dreams, and thrashed young stallions who came neighing at the door, tossing their heads in pride, ready to trample your spirit.

He has displayed his power as a father upon the battlefields of your life as he rode the winds of time. Have you never heard him baying at the moon, commanding it to shine silver moonbeams for you to dance upon? Have you never seen him gather stars from the velvet skies for you to blow wishes upon or watched him lasso rainbows to color your world? Think back—you had only to beckon and he was there.

He has grown weary battling for his maiden, and now he is faced with the man you say you love, while in his mind, this

guy might be Darth Vader in full armor. Dad is very uncertain about the ability of this man, or anyone for that matter, to take care of you better than he has, and quite frankly, he really doesn't want anyone to. You are asking your knight to not only step aside, but you also want him to smile as he turns you over to this masked villain.

You know your intended, but your dad might only see an opponent—one who is lacking in many areas, as far as he is concerned. As always, your dad will follow true to form and move heaven and earth to fulfill your wishes. A valiant knight he is, and one who will walk nobly down the aisle with you, the most precious thing he has, on his arm. Yes, he will plaster a big ole smile on his face to make you happy, because he doesn't want his vulnerability visible to his opponent, your intended.

How do you make your dad feel needed? Meet him for lunch, and ask him to do one very special job for your wedding. You know what he is capable of, so be creative. Maybe ask him to buy the flowers you will have in the room where you plan to dress the day of your wedding, or have him purchase a diary for you to record your feelings through the first months of marriage. Let him know he is still needed and loved.

Father, *thank You for my dad. Help me to understand what he is going through and to reassure him I will always need him. Give me the right words to let him know he is my anchor throughout this stormy wedding, and please keep Your hand of protection on him. Fill the void in others who have never experienced a father's love.*

GRATEFUL THOUGHTS OF MY DAD

DAY 38

Sibling Separation

Your partners in crime are worried.

One of the two which heard John speak, and followed him, was Andrew, Simon Peter's brother. He first findeth his own brother Simon, and saith unto him, We have found the Messias, which is, being interpreted, the Christ. And he brought him to Jesus. And when Jesus beheld him, he said, Thou art Simon the son of Jona: thou shalt be called Cephas, which is by interpretation, A stone.

—John 1:40–42

This is a time of great joy for you, but understand, your siblings may be experiencing severe anxiety. If they seem a little testy, it may be because the relationship they have had with you is going to change—or so they think. The months preceding a wedding are jam-packed with relationship dynamics that are rapidly changing; this is another part of the process that is not just about you.

Memories of all you have ever shared are bombarding your siblings. As far as they are concerned, some unfamiliar guy has maneuvered his way into their family and kidnapped their best friend. In fact, their thoughts would probably surprise you. You are going gaga over those adorable wedding favors, and your siblings are stuck back in time, years ago, remembering how you all used to secretly open your Christmas packages and retape them before your mom and dad found out. You're planning your honeymoon, and all they can think about are the great summer

vacations your family used to take. You remember those don't you? Your dad would go over a checklist that required an Excel spreadsheet, while your mom packed the cooler with all kinds of road trip goodies like Twinkies, soft drinks, and those infernal raisins. Then there was the melodic chanting, "He touched me," "She's on my side of the seat," and the legendary, "I get the window."

Your siblings are worried they are losing you, and in a way, they are. You will never again have the exact same relationship. They are concerned you will emotionally move away from them. Your camaraderie and presence, which was always a guarantee, now appear to be limited by what "that guy" wants.

What to do? Just be sensitive to those who love you, and realize they are having a difficult time with all of this. Reassure them that you are not going anywhere by verbally telling them how important they are to you; don't assume they already know it. Everything really will be OK once they hear that you have not forgotten about them.

Father, *thank You for family. Let me have a knowing heart toward those who have been instrumental in shaping who I am today. Let nostalgia tenderly carry me as I backtrack through my childhood. Thank You for my wonderful heritage.*

THOUGHTS OF CHILDHOOD

DAY 39

How to Handle the Guilt

You're feeling torn, but love can mend it.

A double minded man is unstable
in all his ways.
—James 1:8

Do you feel the pressure all around you? Rejoice, it's not because your clothes are too tight from a sudden weight gain; the pressure is from all the pushing, prodding, and pulling that's going on in your life. That invisible straitjacket you are wearing has you all tied up, laced in manipulative emotions that won't turn you loose. Mom wants you to call her more often, your boss is getting upset with you cruising the wedding sites on the Web, and your intended wants to go one hour without discussing the wedding.

It's no wonder your thoughts are as mixed up as a handful of Scrabble tiles. You can't seem to put words together that spell anything that makes sense. The pressure on you would make F–16 pilots jealous of your ability to withstand so much G force.

What's causing all the pressure? That's easy. You have lost yourself along the way. What you wanted and set out to do has become entangled in all the conflicting desires, and that has

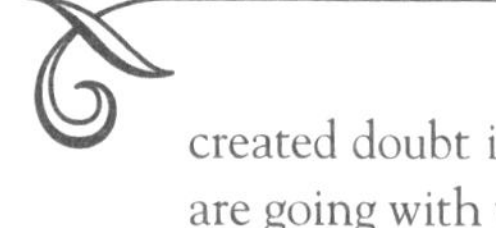

created doubt in your mind. Once you reestablish where it is you are going with your wedding plans, you will feel the pressure ease. Now is not the time to worry about how you can make everything all right for everybody. Frankly, you don't have the patience or expertise to deal individually with everyone else's emotions.

If you stay on track and handle yourself with self-confidence, you will ward off those emotional arrows. You, as the bride, should be very careful not to fall into the trap. Don't use your position as the bride to manipulate people into doing what you want. But don't let yourself be manipulated either. Feelings of guilt are not pleasant, and they have a way of planting themselves in your heart and taking root. Guilt develops a life of its own, and it feeds on bitterness and strife. So give your mom a big kiss and tell her no. It's OK; she loves you. Ahhh, do you feel that corset loosening already? Now, breathe...breathe...breathe.

Father, *thank You for giving me the strength to establish who I am. It is important for me to begin making my own grown-up decisions about what I want from life and where I want my life to go. Help me ward off unmerited guilt and have the wisdom to call it what it is.*

THOUGHTS OF SPIRITUAL GROWTH

COMBINING HOUSEHOLDS

But where do all your shoes go?

That I may cause those that love me to inherit substance; and I will fill their treasures.

—Proverbs 8:21

Along with all the wedding to-dos, you must also think about combining your two households. You may already have experience with this from your college days, but believe me, this is going to be a whole different ball game.

You might have to pick and choose which of those 50 pairs of shoes are going to make it through the cut. Those bulging boxes of purses may have to be whittled down to one purse per month, versus one per week. Uh huh, I'm talking about all those earthly possessions the Bible speaks of; well, some have got to go. Do you really need 30 pairs of panties and 18 pairs of jeans? When you add in his shoes, jeans, and tower of T-shirts, you are talking about a whole lot of clothes.

Next, you have to consider all the other stuff: his sports paraphernalia, high school trophies, Sports Illustrated collection, and Xbox equipment (a trailer load). Couple that with your lotions that would fill a wheel barrel, your stuffed animals that could fill

a Coney Island booth, and your crate of memories you've carted around since you were 16, and you've got a mess.

You don't want friends to walk into your new home and see only one personality displayed. When you enter a living space, a soul should be reflected in what you see. If you walk into a home and see a guitar, you assume someone loves music. If you see photos displayed, you might think someone living there loves photography. The key is to have a little of you and a little of him. You each need some space to use at your own discretion. When you both see items reflecting who you are, you will both feel more at home. It's comforting for you to see the old clock your grandmother gave you, and it's reassuring for your intended to snuggle his hand into his old baseball mitt or see his father's dented toolbox. To make room for some nostalgic items with value in their memories, you have to let some of those snappy sandals go.

Father, *thank You for showing me the things that are important in life. It is great to have possessions, but it's even better to know I recognize the difference between things and heavenly treasures. Where my treasures are, there may my heart be also.**

*See Matthew 6:21 and Luke 12:34.

Thoughts of What's Really Important

· DAY 41 ·

IN-LAWS

Don't let them become outlaws.

And Ruth said, Intreat me not to leave thee, or to return from following after thee: for whither thou goest, I will go; and where thou lodgest, I will lodge: thy people shall be my people, and thy God my God.

—Ruth 1:16

In-laws. You gotta love them! His mom is upset because she has not been listed on the wedding invitations, and your mom can't understand why your mate's father is insisting on a polka dance because of an old family tradition. This is only the beginning, and you can make or break your relationship with his family right here. Whatever you do will set a precedent for your entire married life, so each issue must be dealt with carefully and sensitively.

It will make life easier if you can put yourself in someone else's shoes. Your mate is someone's baby. His mother gave him life, showed him how to tie his shoes, cried when he went off to his first day of school, and nursed him when he was sick. He is, and always will be, her baby. She is fighting to maintain a spot in his life.

Take time to let her know that your new place in his life will not usurp her position. Let her know what a wonderful child she

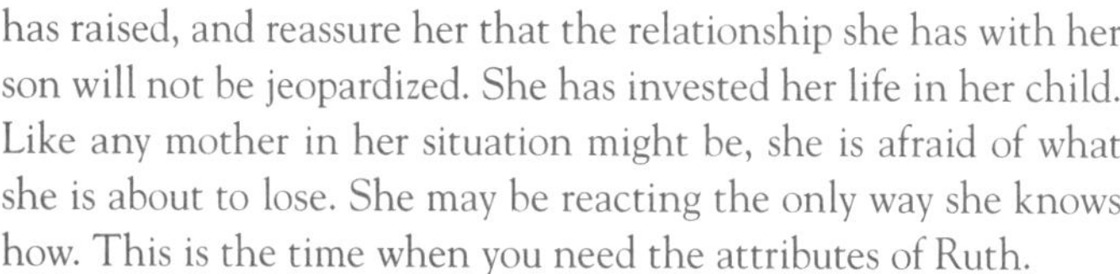

has raised, and reassure her that the relationship she has with her son will not be jeopardized. She has invested her life in her child. Like any mother in her situation might be, she is afraid of what she is about to lose. She may be reacting the only way she knows how. This is the time when you need the attributes of Ruth.

If you don't fully understand now, you will when you have a child of your own and are feeling vulnerable. This situation calls for grace and understanding, but you are up to it. However, times may come when there is no dealing with relatives because they will not change or accept you. In this case, go to your knees before the Lord. He will instruct you on how to conduct yourself in these situations, because He alone knows the hearts of men.

In the meantime, if you are blessed to have in-laws who love you, you should accept them as your own family and give them the same respect and latitude you do your own family. Become one with them; if you can do this, you will never lack for family support. Now, put those loaded words back in your holster, plaster a smile on your face, and wrap your arms around his family.

Father, *I thank You for family. I know the irritation I feel with my future husband's family must be resolved; I just don't know how to do it. Help me to understand how important family is to my mate, and give me strength to hold back negative words, smile, and accept his family as my own.*

DAY 42

SECRETS

It's time to take off the makeup.

The secret things belong unto the L*ORD our God: but those things that are revealed belong unto us and to our children for ever, that we may do all the words of this law.*

—Deuteronomy 29:29

Secrets may have been delicious when you were young, but they can become poisonous as you grow older. What do I mean by that? There were many instances in the Bible in which people secretly did things that put lives in jeopardy. When Jacob gathered his wives, Leah and Rachel, and his belongings and left Laban, his wives' father, Rachel stole her father's images (sacred idols) and hid them among her things. When Laban came after Jacob, Jacob spoke these words, "*With whomsoever thou findest thy gods, let him not live: before our brethren discern thou what is thine with me, and take it to thee. For Jacob knew not that Rachel had stolen them*" (Genesis 31:32). Since Jacob did not know Rachel had stolen the images, he literally pronounced a death sentence over her life.

As your wedding day approaches, your thinking needs to turn to the life you are going to lead and the fact you will now begin to spiritually battle through life together. Your intended needs to

know things of importance—things that could and will affect your lives. Don't leave opportunities for the enemy to blindside him.

Those skeletons rattling around in your closet must come out. With all those clothes, there really isn't room for the skeletons anyway. You want to enter your new life uninhibited, fearless, and with no anxiety. Now's the time to clean up your temple. Hang out all that dirty laundry!

If you truly trust your love, then you should not be afraid to show him parts of yourself that you've kept hidden, whether from shame, fear, or apprehension. The things you have kept safely covered up for so long need to be dragged out, dusted off, and aired out. You should feel safe enough with your intended that you can tell him anything. He may not be able to fix it, but he can sure tote some of that weight you've been carrying.

It is paramount in your married life that you, as a couple, have the freedom to have marital secrets that are not broadcast to your families or friends. Don't expose your Achilles' heel to anyone or give the enemy any ammunition to strike you at your weakest points. Secrets within your marriage will create intimacy.

OK, that's enough seriousness for now. The secrets are exposed. Now put some makeup on to cover up your blushing, and let's get back to planning a wedding!

Father, *I love Your Word, which provides everything I can and will ever need in life. The examples You give in the Bible are little road maps I can use to avoid land mines that could bring destruction and unhappiness into my life. I love meeting You in the secret place, a place where I can pour out my heart and trust You with it all.*

Thoughts of Secrets

WEEK SEVEN

• *Wedding Tips* •

Checklist: Discuss ideas with your officiant. Write thank-you notes as gifts arrive. Have programs printed. Make an appointment for blood tests (if your state requires them), and obtain marriage license and certified copies. If changing your name, get the necessary documents, and send change of address information to the post office.

• • •

Consider this wonderful gesture of love for your moms: Carry two special flowers in your bouquet. As you walk down the aisle, give your mother a kiss and one of the flowers. After the ceremony, as you walk back up the aisle, stop and give your mother-in-law a kiss and a flower.

DAY 43

Heeding the Voice of God

Listen for His voice, rather than the caterer's.

And the LORD called Samuel again the third time. And he arose and went to Eli, and said, Here am I; for thou didst call me. And Eli perceived that the LORD had called the child.... And the LORD came, and stood, and called as at other times, Samuel, Samuel. Then Samuel answered, Speak; for thy servant heareth.

—1 Samuel 3:8, 10

Many voices are speaking right now, and it's hard to clear your mind enough to hear anything. Your caterer is pressuring you to choose between salmon and halibut, your hairdresser wants a time confirmed for your appointment, and the hotel is demanding more information about the rooms you booked for your guests. Are you so stressed out that the Lord has to call you four times, as He did Samuel, before He gets your attention?

He is not going to speak to you from a cloud of white meringue, and He's not going to thunder from that mountain of wedding invitations. When He speaks to you, it will be a whisper in your heart. He is not intrusive; He wants you to invite Him in.

Have you ever been speaking to someone and noticed their eyes roaming all over the place? Even though they kept nodding their head as if in agreement, you knew they were not listening

to what you were saying, and it was very offensive. If you want communion with the Lord, then you need to give Him your undivided attention.

To hear Him speak, you must make time for Him. He is a loving Father, and He does not make appointments, but He is also God. Look at it this way. How much time do you think Donald Trump or the President of the United States would give to you? Now if you were lucky enough to have their undivided attention, do you think they would continue to give you their valuable counsel if they saw your eyes darting all around or had to wait while you answered your cell phone? I think they would probably get up, shake your hand, and tell you to come back when you had ears to hear and time to listen to what they had to say.

The Lord always has time for us. In times of crisis or turmoil, it is difficult to make our souls calm down, take our eyes off of the circumstances, and look toward the heavens for answers. It takes a disciplined mind and a determination to seek and wait until the answers come. We must still ourselves.

Even now, be still. Do you feel that softness cloaking you, that gentleness rippling over you? I told you, He's here!

Father, *thank You for always listening to the voices of Your children. Forgive me for being so embroiled in this wedding that I have neglected Your voice as You called to me. This day I say, as did Samuel, Speak, Lord; for Your servant hears.*

DAY 44

WEDDING JITTERS

This too shall pass.

And it shall be, when thou shalt hear a sound of going in the tops of the mulberry trees, that then thou shalt go out to battle: for God is gone forth before thee to smite the host of the Philistines.

—1 Chronicles 14:15

You started out with a picture of what you wanted your wedding to be, and now it seems like you're holding a box containing a thousand puzzle pieces. You wonder how everything will ever come together. If you've ever put a puzzle together, you know that all those tiny pieces will eventually make a beautiful picture, but it takes time and patience to construct it. Look at the work you have done so far on your wedding. You have an agenda, the place, the time, and most importantly, the guy, so now it's all about the details.

It might help to know you are not alone in your frustration. Over 2.4 million brides are in the same position, and this phenomenon repeats itself every year. See, you're not the only chicken running around without a head; but you may have fooled yourself into thinking you are the only one who may possibly fail at pulling off a wedding. Not so. Whether or not every detail comes off as you would like, the important thing

is that you are going to be married, so take time to enjoy these special moments.

Remember David. As he was going to war, don't you think he was just a wee bit anxious? I'm sure he was going over a hundred details: were his warriors prepared, did he plan for everything that might possibly go wrong, were they adequately armed, and was he really capable of pulling off a mighty victory? Lives depended on his organization and composure; but more importantly, they depended on his having heard instructions from the Lord.

David had to wait until he heard the troops over the mulberry trees; now that's cutting it really close. But regardless of what he saw or felt, even though he had no guarantee of the outcome, he had faith in his God. You can have faith, too.

All of those puzzle pieces for your wedding are going to come together. If you want to see the hand of God and how He has been there each step of the way, look behind you. Do you see all the little mishaps He fixed? Today, get very still, and listen for the sound softly blowing through your life. Is that the "Wedding March" I hear tinkling through the air?

Father, *I know You are Lord of everything. Please take all the pieces of my wedding, and pull them all together. I hear the sounds of life blowing through the trees around me. I can't see You, but I feel You and know You are here. Thank You for Your presence and active participation in these wedding plans.*

DAY 45

You Want to Strangle Your Mom!

But don't! She only wants the best for you.

After this he went down to Capernaum, he, and his mother, and his brethren, and his disciples: and they continued there not many days.

—John 2:12

Here we are discussing your mom again! Are you sorry she learned how to utilize the speed dial feature on her cell phone? But let's take a step back and look at the last few months from her perspective. She loves spending all this time with you, even though she has to walk on eggshells to get to you. Yes, you have been a little temperamental. Luckily, your mom is used to your emotions and moods.

In the New Testament, you will read many times about Jesus's mother being with him. She was at the wedding and in the crowds listening to Him teach, and after He was gone, she still hung out with the guys who walked with Him. She traveled with Him on His journey, and He respected her, as evidenced by the place He gave her in His life.

Your mom has always been with you, too. She was there when you were burning up with fever and felt miserable, she comforted you when the kids made fun of you in school, and it was

she who would have hog-tied any guy who touched one precious hair on your head. Well, all those protective, loving instincts she has cannot magically disappear just because you are not in the mood for them. Her need to touch you and make everything all right has not diminished. Believe me, she is already restraining herself. Look at her clenched hands and those worried wrinkles on her forehead.

You have to give her some credit. You can't have it both ways; either she remains your mom or she doesn't. Either way, you've gotta love her. You might really check yourself, too, and make sure you are not dumping on her, because she is the only one around who will let you.

Over the years, your mom has managed to organize your birthday parties, coordinate your school dance ensembles, and direct you on your life's path, so she does have some wonderful skills you can draw on. She has also accumulated a lot of wisdom, which frankly, you don't have yet. So take your hands off her neck, and wrap your arms around her. Give your mom a big old hug, and take her out to lunch! Her love is invaluable to you.

Father, *thank You for moms. Only You could have known the enormous patience moms would need to support their unconditional love for their children. Sometimes I take that precious love for granted. Today I ask You to let me see my mom in a new light and help me show her my appreciation for her unfailing love.*

DAY 46

FINANCIAL CONCERNS

Do you have to leave those designer jeans behind?

And the Lord said, Who then is that faithful and wise steward,
whom his lord shall make ruler over his household,
to give them their portion of meat in due season?
—Luke 12:42

Through this wedding experience, you are getting a taste of how quickly money can vanish. Suddenly those bridesmaid bouquets look just as good with carnations as they did with roses. See how quickly you can make adjustments! Budgets really are your friends, though we tend to look at them as ogres that slap our fingers every time we forget that five dollars minus eight dollars leaves us a negative three dollars. Now you understand what happened to your bank account when you purchased that new leather jacket!

Following a budget will help you keep your emotions intact and balanced. Nothing can put the fire out on a hot, steamy romance quicker than money problems. Here are some red flags signaling an impending financial disaster: In your mind, have ATMs become diabolical robots that are eating your money? Has the mailbox transformed itself into a fire-breathing dragon that blasts out bills like flames each time you open it, or is it

like a crazed popcorn machine, popping out more bills than you can handle? Has your checkbook developed a voice only you can hear—one that laughs every time you open it? If you've answered yes to any of these questions, then you must begin to assert power over your money before it devours you.

One of the major causes of divorce is financial woes. If you ever experience them and see how controlling such woes can be, you'll understand. The Bible says love never fails; but let me tell you, money woes come pretty close to smothering the life out of love. You've heard the slogan, "there is nothing between me and my jeans," right? Well dip your hand too often into your intended's pocket, and you've just gotten between a man and his jeans! Your smiling, soft-spoken man will turn on you like a rabid chipmunk.

Designer jeans and T-shirts adorned with well-known logos don't have to be a thing of the past. They may fit very nicely into your new budget, right above the line where you have reduced your movie rental bill. A budget will make everything fit. Unfortunately, it's like losing weight: something's got to come off before more can go in. Now look behind you. Do you see the Lord smiling? No, He isn't looking at that designer label on your back; He's looking at your smiling face and loving it.

Father, *thank You for setting standards of excellence for Your people. I know You want the best for me, and the best for me includes becoming a good steward of what You have given me. Thank You again for blessings and the wisdom to utilize them.*

THOUGHTS ON BUDGETING

DAY 47

SEXUAL INTIMACY

Touching is essential.

Let him kiss me with the kisses of his mouth:
for thy love is better than wine.
—Song of Solomon 1:2

Ever since you were a little girl, touch has been a way of communication: a pat on the head, a cool hand on your fevered brow, and a gentle brush upon your cheek always brought you peace and comfort. A touch has the amazing ability to heal, soothe, and make everything OK.

I know you are very busy with wedding plans—you have to make your hair appointment and book your honeymoon. But take time also to stay in touch with the one you love. Tempers may have flared a little, some tears of frustration probably have been shed, and you may wonder if you are going to make it through this whole ordeal.

Your love is clamoring for the "old you," so give it to him and remind him that he is special. Make time for him, and forget about the caterers and corsages for a while. No matter how in love you feel, it is very easy to neglect the needs of one another. Touching is what reconnects you.

Behind closed doors is a world that belongs to lovers. It's where florescent lights are forgotten, giving way to the mellow light of vanilla candles. Gas fumes and honking horns are replaced by intoxicating perfumes and sultry notes wafting through the air. Harsh voices from work-weary bodies are hushed with soothing words, softly spoken, accompanied by gentle touches. It's a time of private love and secret desires. Deprived of the warm sun touching its petals, the cool earth nourishing its roots, and the dewdrop caress of velvety nights, a beautiful rose will quickly die. Dim the lights, turn the music on, and turn off the cell phone. Ah! Romance.

Intimacy is an important part of your relationship with your mate. This doesn't just happen. You have to turn off the TV and lock the front door. You have to make time, set the mood, and physically shut out the world. Emotional intimacy is necessary for keeping love alive, and you are preparing for the ultimate intimacy of married love. Don't forget the importance of staying in touch with each other—just the two of you.

Father, *please stir me when I get forgetful of my love's needs. Let our relationship be one of give and take, a continual process into the deeper things of love. Help us to reach heights of intimacy as Solomon, where just a kiss makes us whole.*

THOUGHTS OF INTIMACY

DAY 48

WHO IS THIS MAN?

He keeps changing—like Clark Kent in a phone booth.

In a moment, in the twinkling of an eye, at the last trump: for the trumpet shall sound, and the dead shall be raised incorruptible, and we shall be changed.
—1 Corinthians 15:52

Does it seem like your intended has changed over the last few months? Are your conversations a little clipped and your romantic evenings laced with just a hint of irritation? Are you questioning his ability to understand you?

Well, he might not be poring over caterer menus or scouring discount shops for gift bag items, but he does have his own concerns and worries. You might wonder what in the world he could possibly be worried about, since it is obvious you are doing all the work. (I hear that whine; let's save the violins for the reception.)

He is wondering what his new role will be. His carefree days of tossing football jerseys on the floor, owning the remote control, and eating pizza for breakfast are threatened. His prize vehicle's glove compartment looks like the makeup counter of a drugstore, and his magazines are being tossed in the trash before he has taken his usual three months to read them. He witnesses the full brunt of your tongue as you lash out at inept wedding planners

and not-too-bright florists. He is seeing you at the extremes of your emotional range, and he doesn't know how to deal with it. Should he be gentle and try to soothe you, or should he get angry along with you? These turbulent waters he is navigating are forcing him to change as quickly as a chameleon, and he is not used to it. The man you see—the one who seems to keep changing—is probably just trying to keep up with your mood swings.

It sounds too easy, but most men will be forever happy if you feed them a meatloaf sandwich, pop some chocolate chip cookies out of the oven every month or so, and keep plenty of toilet paper in the bathroom. This might not be politically correct, but it's the honest truth: men are not complicated beings. Your man's confusion will dissipate once he recognizes what his responsibilities are going to be. Like it or not, you are considered his space now. He feels an inward inclination to protect and take care of you; he just hasn't figured out what all that will entail.

Now is the time to reassure him that he is up to the job and nothing is going to change too drastically. Promise him that if he hangs on for a few more months, you will amply reward him with some of those delicious cookies. See how quickly he turned back into his old self? Just look at that smile!

Father, *thank You that you have made us flexible and able to change. I want to really look at my love and try to understand what he is feeling. If he is uncertain or scared, give me the words to say that will bring peace into his heart. Above all, let me see him smile.*

DAY 49

LISTENING BEYOND THE WORDS

There's a heart in there.

A good man out of the good treasure of his heart bringeth forth that which is good; and an evil man out of the evil treasure of his heart bringeth forth that which is evil: for of the abundance of the heart his mouth speaketh.

—Luke 6:45

Communication is vital for a successful relationship. How many times have you heard, "He's not hearing what I'm saying"? There is a very simple explanation for this, and if you can get this concept, you will be miles ahead of most women. Men have an instinctive need to "fix" everything. They don't understand that the majority of the time, all you really want is someone to listen while you vent.

The reason he doesn't hear you is because as soon as you begin to relate a problem, he immediately clicks into the "fix it" mode and is busily trying to come up with a solution to your dilemma. This is why most of the time when they themselves are the problem, your words just seem to fly right over their heads. In their minds, how can you fix something that isn't broke? Now do you see how hilarious this whole thing can get?

You can be ranting on and on about how the dress shop wants to charge you extra for your alterations, but the root of

the matter is that you are worried about finances. If you had an unlimited wedding budget, you wouldn't give the additional charges a second thought. You need to go deeper than the words being spoken to develop communication skills that will create an intimate relationship with the man you love.

Let's say your fiancé is giving you some negative feedback on the guest list. You know him well enough to understand that he wouldn't give a flip about two extra guests. So what is the real problem? You will probably find out some relative has been complaining to his mom about how Joe, his eighth cousin removed, has not received an invitation. If you are listening, you will know his words do not align with his heart. Instead of getting frustrated with him over the guest list, start digging deeper. Find the problem.

You will discover the heart of the one you love is grounded in love, wanting only the best for you. His words may not be eloquent and words might come tumbling out of his mouth at the wrong time in the wrong place, but consider the intent. Look into his eyes, watch his body language, and listen with your heart to what he is really saying. Give him a break…I mean, a whole lot of breaks. That's the only way you will be able to successfully keep a line of communication open between yourselves. He must be able to trust you and know that even if he errs, you will understand his true intention.

Father, *help me see the hidden man of the heart in the one I love. Allow me to peer into his eyes, the windows of his soul, and see into the depths of him. Give me ears to hear what he is really saying, and let me never get so lax that I fail to take the time to listen beyond his words.*

THINGS HE HAS TOLD ME

Week Eight

• *Wedding Tips* •

Checklist: Contact local newspapers about publishing the wedding announcement. Check on your new home requirements: leases, moving arrangements, electricity, water, phone, cable, and insurance. Make arrangements for someone to be responsible for getting your gifts from the reception to your new location and for someone to return the men's formal wear, if they are rented.

• • •

To create a special memory, plan at least one wedding day surprise for your mate. He has heard every detail of your plans, so he knows what to expect. Let there be something unexpected just for him! Have your guests sing the fight song of his old school, make a mini cake of his favorite hobbies or sports, or secretly invite an old friend of his. Make it an unforgettable day for him.

DAY 50

WHO DOES GOD SAY YOU ARE?

It's not your Social Security number.

Thus saith the LORD, thy redeemer, and he that formed thee from the womb, I am the LORD that maketh all things; that stretcheth forth the heavens alone; that spreadeth abroad the earth by myself.

—Isaiah 44:24

All your life, you have been categorized. Think about it. You've been someone's daughter, someone's sister, the moody one or the funny one, the neat freak or the Messy Marvin of the family. A sign on your desk at work denotes your position, you snap to attention when your number is called at the deli, and you jump through hoops when the government investigates your number. In all your uniqueness, how in the world did you get lost in this huge sea of humanity? Does anyone really know who *you* are?

Yes. One does. One knows every hair on your head and every bone in your body. He's the One who created you for His enjoyment, and He wants nothing from you but your love and fellowship. If you want to cry on His shoulder because this whole wedding mess has gotten out of control, that's OK. If you decide to stamp your feet and threaten to elope, He'll be there, too. Why? Because He loves you and has faith in you!

We are talking about the Creator who knit your bones together while you were still in the womb. If you don't know what God says about you, now is a good time to find out. (See Psalm 139:1–6, 13–16.)

When you are full of righteous anger, He says, "Watch out, kingdom of darkness, because when she develops and directs that force toward you, she will storm the gates of hell in My name." Do you have a heart as big as Texas? He smiles and says, "With all that compassion, she will be an extension of My love toward those who are hurting." What about that contagious smile of yours? He's banking on you using it to bring hope to others whose worlds have become shrouded in darkness.

Ponder all the little traits you have and embrace the whole of who God says you are. Now, some of your characteristics may require some nipping and tucking, and many still need to mature. All in all, you are the special, unique creation He fashioned for His purpose.

You may be just a number to the IRS, but the Lord created you in such totality that at the sound of the trumpet, He is going to collect each and every molecule of your body and reconstruct you all over again. Now that ought to tell you something. It seems He's content with you just the way you are!

Father, *thank You for caring about me. It's wonderful to know that in this vast world, I can raise my voice to You in prayer and You hear it. Among all the voices, You alone listen to me perfectly. What an awesome God You are!*

Thoughts on God's Creation

DAY 51

PICK YOUR BATTLES

You're not out to conquer.

And he said, Hearken ye, all Judah, and ye inhabitants of Jerusalem, and thou king Jehoshaphat, Thus saith the LORD unto you, Be not afraid nor dismayed by reason of this great multitude; for the battle is not yours, but God's.

—2 Chronicles 20:15

If you get upset about petty things, you are considered temperamental; if you rarely go against the grain and have an easygoing attitude, you're called temperate. What's the difference? It all depends on if you really aspire to be that "Proverbs 31" woman, or if you're satisfied with just winning.

Sometimes little issues will arise; be willing to let those go. Then when big issues—the ones that truly affect you—come up, you can take a stand. If you insist that every minor decision go your way, how will anyone know what is really important to you?

Warring requires strategy, planning, and manipulation. Do you really want to expend all that energy just to have your mom wear an ecru-colored dress instead of that cream-colored one she loves? If your intended has not made any requests for the wedding, and then asks to have his college football fight song played as you both enter the reception, obviously it is important to him. He has let you have everything you wanted; so if he makes one

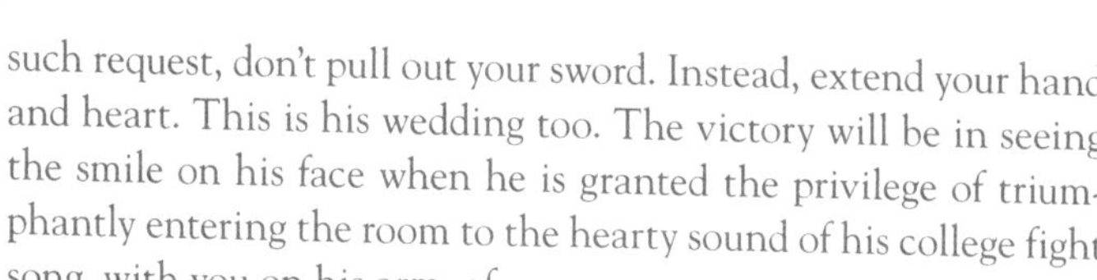

such request, don't pull out your sword. Instead, extend your hand and heart. This is his wedding too. The victory will be in seeing the smile on his face when he is granted the privilege of triumphantly entering the room to the hearty sound of his college fight song, with you on his arm, of course.

Now, if he wants the kitchen cabinets arranged like his mother always did, it's time to pick up your sword. His request has now entered your space and hit a nerve. This is a matter of the heart. You naturally want to establish yourself as the woman of the house, and some issues will be worth fighting for.

For a relationship to thrive, it is vital that neither of you give up your *voice*. Dictatorships are created when one person believes he or she has all knowledge and wisdom. Democracies are established when all views are considered before a joint decision is made. Never lose sight of the power you have when you pull together. The Bible refers to one putting a thousand to flight and two putting ten thousand to flight when the Lord is at work (see Deuteronomy 32:30). Remember who the enemy is. Your loved one is *not* the enemy. Jesus told us Satan has come to kill, steal, and destroy, so redirect those fiery darts toward the right target and not each other.

Father, *thank You for providing in Your Word all the wisdom I need. Help me acquire a better understanding of how to rightly confront conflict in my marriage. All my days, be by my side to help me differentiate the important from the trivial, and give me the grace to let the trivial issues go.*

Thoughts of Healthy Conflict

DAY 52

Spiritual Authorities

The mantle is changing.

And he took the mantle of Elijah that fell from him, and smote the waters, and said, Where is the L*ORD God of Elijah? And when he also had smitten the waters, they parted hither and thither: and Elisha went over.*

—2 Kings 2:14

The Scripture above is a snapshot of what is going to occur when you say, "I do." A mantle can best be described as "spiritual authority" or "power of attorney." If you were blessed enough to have parents who served the Lord, then you have had prayer warriors constantly seeking an audience with the Lord on your behalf. Their prayers prevented many mishaps in your life and brought supernatural peace to you in times of trouble. They were the Elijahs, and now your beloved will be the Elisha.

Your parents may be a little apprehensive about your marriage because they realize a shifting of power is about to take place. They are not quite sure your young man is up to the task of providing you spiritual cover. He may be a great provider and may see to your every whim, but is he up to seeking the heart of God for both of you?

Your husband will play such an important role in your life that he will have a part in every decision you make for the rest of

your life. You need him to be the kind of man who consistently seeks the Lord's will for both of your lives. However, don't think he will get all the blame if something goes wrong, because you have a vital part to play in this. You, as his confidant and friend, are to provide your husband wise counsel and prayer cover. What does that all mean?

It means that throughout your married life, you will be responsible for providing protection for your husband in the spirit world. As he charges ahead in prayer, he will need someone covering his back—and that someone is you! Through days of sickness, financial distress, and worry, it will be the prayers of the saints and a personal relationship with the Lord that will bring you deliverance.

Now do you see why your parents are so concerned about the choice you made? They must turn over their role in your protection to another, and they are already feeling the balance of power shifting. They will always have a prayerful say in your life, but ultimately, your husband will be the one closest alongside you, seeking the Lord's will on bended knees. So drag out your shield of faith, plop on that helmet of salvation, and take up the sword of the Spirit (the Word of God); your beloved needs some cover!

Father, *thank You for giving me a husband to care spiritually for me. I will try to understand what is required of me in this huge spiritual change, and I will work with my mate to wage war that Your will may be done here on earth, as it is in heaven.**

*See Matthew 6:10.

THOUGHTS OF OUR SPIRITUAL RELATIONSHIP

· DAY 53 ·

PRAYING TOGETHER

Weld your souls.

Likewise, husbands, live with your wives in an understanding way,
showing honor to the woman as the weaker vessel,
since they are heirs with you of the grace of life,
so that your prayers may not be hindered.
—1 Peter 3:7 (ESV)

"Weaker vessel?" OK, I can feel your hackles rising. Wait a minute. The Word of God says that there is neither Jew nor Greek, neither male nor female (see Galatians 3:28). No distinction is shown in that Scripture Paul penned; so obviously, the Lord has a different interpretation of "weaker vessel" than we do.

Women see the splendor of sunsets, love the sweet scent of roses, and melt at a baby's touch. For most women, emotions are the cornerstone of life. At the same time, our compassion and ability to feel our way through life make us vulnerable. These characteristics can be both a tremendous strength and a weakness. At times, our emotions need to take a backseat to practical matters; that is when you need to let the practical one do the leading.

There will be times of crisis when you have to put your feelings aside, listen to wise counsel, and forge ahead on the

information you have been provided. Other times, your heart will speak louder than any facts and will lead you with the inner witness, which makes no sense at all. It is just a feeling that "this is the way to go, walk ye in it" (see Isaiah 30:21).

Decisions need to be made together, prayerfully. Your mate's wisdom and your heart's tugging should be used jointly in your effort to pull down strongholds that try to deter you from achieving all God has for you. It is important that you both immediately establish a ritual of praying together. Your souls will become fused, and you will begin to pull in the same direction, having the same desires and goals.

When you seek the Lord, it is important to know you both are asking for the same thing. You don't want to be praying for household finances and hear your mate praying for a new sports car. Praying together provides a check and balance system.

Father, *please bless our prayer life, and give us the tenacity to always seek Your face together, united before You. I want our life to revolve around You. May we always be in a state of grace, able to approach Your throne, washed in righteousness.*

THOUGHTS OF PRAYER

DAY 54

WARFARE IS NECESSARY

But no warfare is allowed in the bedroom.

Then he said to me, Fear not, Daniel, for from the first day that you set your heart to understand and humbled yourself before your God, your words have been heard, and I have come because of your words. The prince of the kingdom of Persia withstood me twenty-one days, but Michael, one of the chief princes, came to help me, for I was left there with the kings of Persia, and came to make you understand what is to happen to your people in the latter days. For the vision is for days yet to come.

—Daniel 10:12–14 (ESV)

You have made a commitment to a man to whom you believe the Lord is joining you. However, there is one who is in direct opposition to anything the Lord would have, and that is Satan. As you read above, Daniel's prayers were heard the first time he prayed, but it took 21 days for the messenger of the Lord to reach him. Michael waged war against other angels, so the messenger could bring the answer to Daniel. And you know, time has not changed the way spiritual warfare takes place.

Cell phones, fax machines, and computers have not hindered the kingdom of darkness. Our way of doing things differs from that of years ago, but spiritual laws have been established since the beginning of time, and like the Lord, they change not. You may not want to believe or acknowledge these facts, but you only

have to open your eyes and your Bible to see that some things that occur on this earth have no logical explanation.

Tiffs between you and your mate will occur; but if an unusual amount of pressure or illogical irritation is present, look for a force larger than you that might be bringing trouble into your life. At the beginning of your relationship, the enemy will try his best to bring destruction, because he knows your marriage will only be as strong as its foundation. Forces will try to destroy the groundwork of your marriage, because if the base can be shaken, then the whole relationship will crumble.

To prevent the enemy from encroaching on what you are building, warfare is necessary, and that warfare is carried out through prayer and seeking the direction of the Lord. Don't allow the fussy *have to's* of your wedding deter you from what is important: the safeguarding of your relationship. Prepare to make a home that is an oasis from the storms of life, and let your love be a haven where war has no place.

Father, *thank You for making us warriors for Your kingdom. I know You would not give me a mission to do without equipping me to do it. Show me how to wage this war, and give me discernment in seeing the distinction between good and evil.*

Thoughts on a Life of Love

55 DAY

HAVING BELIEFS, NOT RELIGION

Theologies may crumble, but foundations bear the weight.

Pure religion and undefiled before God and the Father is this, to visit the fatherless and widows in their affliction, and to keep himself unspotted from the world.

—James 1:27

Throughout this wedding experience, I'm sure you have found this is one time in life when you want the best of everything. You want a quality product, and you allow no room for substitutions. The same can be said of your beliefs. All the Sunday School stories you've heard throughout your life will not sustain you in moments of crisis. God paints the skies with vibrant rainbows and fills valleys with colorful flowers, but where His Word is concerned, He uses pure black and white. You can't find even a hint of gray.

How well He knows man and the depths man will go to stretch His truth, contort His words, and twist the intent of His message. To make it real plain, He drew up a very simple plan and said, "one jot or one tittle shall in no wise pass from the law, till all be fulfilled" (Matthew 5:18). No leeway is allowed.

All He wants from you is for you to believe. You lay a foundation for belief from day-to-day experiences during which you

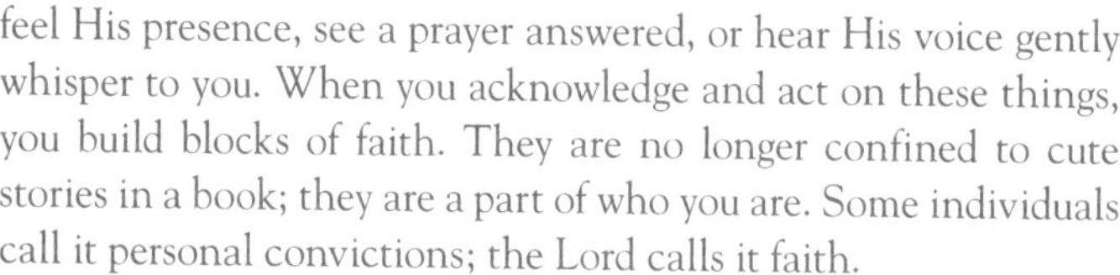

feel His presence, see a prayer answered, or hear His voice gently whisper to you. When you acknowledge and act on these things, you build blocks of faith. They are no longer confined to cute stories in a book; they are a part of who you are. Some individuals call it personal convictions; the Lord calls it faith.

For months, you have thumbed through hundreds of magazines, looking at wedding dresses and thinking about how you would react or feel when you found the right one. Until you added action—put your leg through that swirl of confection puddled on the floor, slid it up your body, and looked at yourself in the mirror—you had only thoughts, mental images, assumptions, and theories of how you would respond at that moment. Staring at that gown in the window was a "maybe" thought, but watching the salesgirl gather up that white frothy dress and pin your name on it made it a reality. Your beliefs come alive through action and application.

Take in the Word one day at a time—absorb it, digest it, and apply it. In days to come, in a moment of dire need, you will be able to pull the Word out of your heart and speak it. You may be afraid, your knees may tremble, your hands may shake, and all logic may point to destruction, but stomp your foot and feel that foundation beneath you—it is Jesus, and He's rock solid.

Father, *thank You for giving me a blueprint for my life. Where I have wandered into gray areas, creating confusion and turmoil, draw me back into black and white. Let me experience the simplicity of Your Word and the foundational strength found in You.*

Thoughts of What I Truly Believe

DAY 56

Be a Doer of the Word

Don't window shop the Word. Own it!

But be ye doers of the word, and not hearers only,
deceiving your own selves.
—James 1:22

Do you remember learning to tie your shoes, riding your first bicycle, and all the other little supposedly simple things that now enable you to actually walk, talk, and chew bubble gum at the same time? You listened to instructions, watched, and then applied what you heard. You could have read books on tying shoes, but until you actually took those laces in your hands and tied your own shoes, they would have been only words on a page.

The same principle applies to the Word of God. The secret to the power of the Word is not so much in memorizing Scriptures; it's in the miracles that occur when you enact what you read.

Some people will be hearers all their lives, never willing to take risks or venture out of their comfort zones. Marriage is a risk because it involves commitment to a life of unknowns. The victory is that you are willing to be a doer. You are betting that life

holds a whole lot more for you, and you're putting your trust in God to bring it to fruition.

Speak a kind word to your caterer or hug your bridesmaid.* Give a touch, a smile, or a word of encouragement to someone who needs it.* When you see the Word come alive in your life, you own it. Simple memorization becomes a thing of the past, and the Word becomes *who* you are. If someone tries to tell you the Word isn't for today, your rock solid beliefs will not be shaken, because you have experienced it!

Open your Bible today, pick a Scripture that speaks to your heart, and enact it. Take the Word off the pages, put it in your mouth, let it flow through the activities of your hands, and direct your feet. You have just become an ambassador of Christ.

Father, *I want to be a doer of Your Word today and all the days of my life. I desire to be an active participant in Your kingdom here on earth. Give me the insight I need to read, understand, and apply Your Word. Confirm the words I read with signs and wonders following. Jesus, thank You for sending the Holy Spirit, the teacher, who shows me all things of You.*

*See Ephesians 4:32; 1 Corinthians 13:4–5; Proverbs 17:22; Romans 12:5–8; and 1 Thessalonians 5:11.

THOUGHTS OF APPLYING THE WORD

WEEK NINE

• *Wedding Tips* •

Checklist: Set up an agenda for the wedding day that includes time for everyone to meet for photos. Assign drivers and cars for the wedding party and family members. Get the cell phone numbers of all who are involved in the wedding, including the photographer, caterer, and florist. Set up an emergency agenda with items needed in case of weather changes, no-shows, or other possible mishaps.

• • •

As you develop your guest list, write each person's full name and address on 3-by-5-inch cards, and place them alphabetized in a card box. Upon receiving a gift, pull the card for that person, and describe the gift on it. When you send your thank-yous, all the needed information is available to include a description of the gift and speedily address your cards.

DAY 57

BECOMING A DOMESTIC DIVA

You've got to find a place for all that stuff.

When I was a child, I spake as a child, I understood as a child,
I thought as a child: but when I became a man,
I put away childish things.
—1 Corinthians 13:11

The gifts are coming in! While you salivate over the beautiful Wedgwood crystal, your beloved is scanning the cache, wondering which container can hold his beef jerky.

Those skills you acquired while playing dress up and popping mud pies out of your pink plastic oven are blossoming. Those dreamy childhood days of poring over the Sears catalog and picking out miniature tea sets and play pots and pans have culminated into what we adults call a gift register, and it's wish day all over again. Can you believe all these presents? It just keeps getting better and better.

All of those wonderful gifts need to go somewhere, and let me clue you in: your mom and dad are not going to want you to take up half their garage to store your belongings. Space can be a real issue when you are first married, because as you combine the yours, mine, and ours, the compilation becomes an ownership headache. The first time you're late for work and find your

love has unplugged the automatic coffeemaker so he could charge up his drill, you will understand.

All your new gadgets need a place to go, and you are likely the one who will be determining placement as you establish a rhythm and order for your home. Your mate doesn't give a flip about where you put the cookie sheets; he just wants to make sure that when they pop out of wherever you hide them, they are soon sizzling with fresh-baked cookies.

Single men usually live in a little disorder, so they are somewhat pliable and may welcome any form of order, as long as you don't begin micromanaging their tools, hiding their sports paraphernalia, or messing with their preset channels on the remote control.

More than just a wedding is taking place; two separate lives are being blended into one unified life that you get to share with your best friend! He will listen when you can't sleep, massage your feet when those three-inch stilettos do you in, and buy Neapolitan ice cream, being sure to save the chocolate part for you.

Father, *thank You for divine order and the ability to change and see beyond my own needs. Please help me organize our home into a place that is comfortable for both of us. I want to make a home that thrives on love and peace—a place where all who enter can sense Your presence, a safe harbor from the world.*

THOUGHTS OF MY NEW LIFE

58 · DAY ·

BUILDING YOUR NEST

Make it sparkle!

And Abram said unto Lot, Let there be no strife, I pray thee, between me and thee, and between my herdmen and thy herdmen; for we be brethren.

—Genesis 13:8

Lot was Abram's nephew and had been traveling with Abram for many years. They had arrived in the land the Lord had promised to Abram and his descendants. Abram and Lot owned so much livestock that the land was unable to contain them as long as they stayed together. To dispel any strife amongst them and their servants, Abram suggested they split up and allowed Lot to pick the section of land he wanted. Needless to say, Lot picked what he thought was the best piece of land. But Abram valued the land as nothing, in order that he might have peace in his life.

How much are you willing to give up to have peace in your new life? You will have to make some huge adjustments. Ah! Woman of the house, you now have your own little kingdom to run. How about that! It's exciting, isn't it? Well, that kingdom comes with some responsibilities, such as food preparation, wise money management, and yes, putting out the garbage, sometimes. Ouch, did Humpty Dumpty just fall off the wall?

How are you going to establish your new life? It's up to you to create a "nest." You'll fall into that role naturally, because the Lord, in all His eternal wisdom, created a homing device in women that from the moment they are born, begins leading them toward a place they call home. It seems to lock onto its site as soon as an engagement ring is slipped on the finger. Suddenly, the woman is Dorothy, who chants to Toto, "There's no place like home. There's no place like home."

Home is a place where you and your mate can escape the world and build a life together. This is a time of discovery—a real awakening as to who you both really are. Jesus was born in a stable and laid in a manger because there was no room for his family in the inn, but that did not alter the power or direction of the Man. You both must be able to find happiness and adapt wherever you are. In no time, you will have that nest built. Look at nature. Both male and female birds may gather the twigs, but do you see that sparkling button or that wayward piece of lint adorning the twigs? That's a mama's way of giving her nest that little sparkle!

Father, *thank You for womanly intuition. I desire to make wherever I live a home, and I know that can only be accomplished through the love and warmth You bring into a relationship. Give me skills and insight beyond my years, and grant me the gift of hospitality so my home will shine with Your love. I pray for those who have no home in which to find rest and peace. Bless those who work with the homeless and downtrodden, and give them strength to do Your work.*

THOUGHTS OF MY NEW HOME

DAY 59

If Your Mate Is Unsaved

Have the patience of Job.

And another angel came out of the temple, crying with a loud voice to him that sat on the cloud, Thrust in thy sickle, and reap: for the time is come for thee to reap; for the harvest of the earth is ripe.

—Revelation 14:15

You treasure the relationship you have with the Lord, and you have come to know Him as a friend and confidant. The same can be said of your relationship with your intended. You may know all about this wonderful man you're going to marry, but your parents, relatives, and friends don't. If your mate is unsaved, it will bring a whole new dimension of concern for him.

If your chosen mate is not a Christian, you are taking on a heaviness in your relationship that will be lightened only when he accepts the salvation God offers through Jesus Christ. Your parents may be concerned about it. You may be concerned about it. Someone may have shared with you the passage urging Christians not to be "unequally yoked" (2 Corinthians 6:14); still you have decided to marry this man. You are certainly not the first Christian to marry an unsaved person, but you take on a solemn responsibility when you do. You must nurture your

own relationship with the Lord without your husband's help, and you must be an example to him, preparing the way for his eventual salvation.

Even if your mate has not met your Lord, he knows you have a relationship with someone special he can't see. He notices how your face lights up when you speak of Him. He hears you praying and can't dispute the fact that no one can calm you down like the Lord. This will intrigue him and may create in him a yearning to meet this "friend" of yours. The Holy Spirit will softly nudge and call him when the time is right.

Have you ever plucked a beautiful orange from a tree only to find the inside is hard, not having had time to mature? The outside looks good, but that does not mean the fruit has ripened. The same goes for the heart of man. The Lord draws a man when his heart is softened and prepared. Babies gestate, dough rests, and fine wine ages. Patience has been portrayed as a heavy thing, and it tends to bring on a big sigh, but there can be extreme beauty and completion when it is enacted.

Your mate will treasure his journey to the Lord. The miracle is him finding that little speck of light in a dark world, where he is lost and making his way as the voice of God directs his steps. Hang on. Be patient. Your mate is the Lord's creation, and He loves him far more than you ever could. Believe He is working in him.

Father, *thank You for Your promise that Your will is for every man to be saved. I ask that ministering spirits surround my loved one and minister to him, for he is an heir of salvation. Give me the assurance that my love and I will both walk upon streets of gold through eternity.*

DAY 60

THE WORD AS A LIFESTYLE

It's not a paperweight.

Ask, and it shall be given you; seek, and ye shall find; knock, and it shall be opened unto you.

—Matthew 7:7

I bet the first thing on your mind this morning and the last thought you had before your head hit the pillow last night were thoughts of your wedding. Wedding planning has become a lifestyle for you. You breathe, speak, and are totally consumed by it. That's OK; that's called being focused. Through that process, you are turning your vision for your wedding into a reality.

If you are a Christian, another lifestyle is also being practiced by you—the lifestyle of your walk with the Lord. Sometime in your past, you came to know the Lord. This discovery may have come about through instruction in a Sunday School class, the testimony of a friend, or a glorious revelation, but you mustn't stop there. Once the experience has passed, many people never venture into an intimate relationship with the Lord. Look around. Do you see people like that sitting in pews each Sunday? They are like paperweights, as cold as stone and just as immovable.

Your relationship with the Lord must never become stagnant; it needs to be constantly evolving. Always ask for more, seek the Lord's face, and knock on the doors of heaven. Use what you learned of Him as a child and build on it, continually propelling yourself forward into a greater understanding of Him. The longer you seek Him, the more intense and exciting the quest. And with all that knocking, He hears you.

How do you become more aware of the Lord—how do you incorporate Him into every area of your life? That's easy: just breathe. He's here. Close your eyes. Do you feel that sweet, comforting flow rippling over you like warm honey? It's Him. When you start your day, take a moment to look at His creation, and give Him thanks. When you can't find your car keys, stop and pray. He knows where they are. When you get a call to inform you the florist has located those pale lavender roses you just had to have for your wedding bouquet, praise Him. These are examples of how He becomes a part of your life, rather than just an entity you religiously pay homage to on Sunday.

Today, if you are experiencing a void inside of you that keeps hinting that there is still one thing missing, fill that void with the Lord. Have breakfast with Him, and He will walk with you all day long.

Father, *I want to keep growing in You. Give me a continuous hunger for more of You, and keep me teachable. Help me to daily see more and more of who You are. With You at the breakfast table with me, I believe I will have the willpower to push aside that luscious cinnamon bun.*

DAY 61

ALWAYS NEED HIM

You don't have to carry the whole load.

And the LORD God caused a deep sleep to fall upon Adam, and he slept: and he took one of his ribs, and closed up the flesh instead thereof; And the rib, which the LORD God had taken from man, made he a woman, and brought her unto the man.

—Genesis 2:21–22

Adam has not gone anywhere; he's just been transformed into that sports jock positioned in front of your TV set. Watch as he frantically screams commands at the video game he's playing while moving the joystick with the speed and precision of an ace pilot. Yes, man has totally evolved. Here he is, and—would you believe it—you need him!

We already know you can do it all, but the secret of a good relationship is the ability to work together. If you continue juggling everything alone, you have no interaction with your mate. When you take on a project, ask his advice, seek his assistance, and listen to what he has to say.

Do everything you can to stay on the same path. You both may pursue your own personal interests, but some common ground is also needed—an interest that draws you together to work toward the same goal. If you do not lure him into a common interest, he will make his own life. In his world, cuddling is replaced with

the recliner, and talking is defined as text messaging. One way to stay connected with him is to set mini goals for yourselves. It may be as simple as planting flowers along your walkway or putting a puzzle together. The concept is to continually set activities in motion that employ talking, touching, and laughing.

Today you are in charge of the wedding details and love it, but a few years down the road when you are balancing a baby on one hip, a bag of groceries on the other, and carrying your car keys in your teeth, you will need help. Why not establish a working relationship right from the start? Always need him, and let him know it. The world may negatively call this need *codependency*; I call it *cooperation!*

Father, *Your Word continually speaks of people needing people, disciples going forth in twos, believers praying one for another, and your presence being where two or three are gathered. Help me to release to my love some of the burden I have been carrying, and show us how to be helpmates for each other.*

• DAY •

Defend One Another

You can discuss it later.

And Jesus knew their thoughts, and said unto them, Every kingdom divided against itself is brought to desolation; and every city or house divided against itself shall not stand.

—Matthew 12:25

No one likes to be picked on; nor is it pleasant to watch it happen to others. Most all of us have seen couples who constantly fight and pick on each other. When this occurs, it makes everyone else uncomfortable. To address the conflict, one rises up in a defensive mode, and that ignites aggression. People arguing or fighting have little control over their emotions, and their words begin to fly uncontrolled—words spew forth that cannot be captured or destroyed. When hurtful words are unleashed, they head straight for the heart and cause lasting wounds. Throwing out an apathetic apology, "Sorry," does not bring healing to overcome the damage hurtful words have created.

The two of you must not react negatively toward each other when you are in public. Individuals who make fun of their mate in public are showing a lack of respect for their partners. It puts the one being attacked into a very vulnerable position. You really don't want this to happen to the one you love.

Defend one another. Always stand determinedly by your mate. If someone is directing criticism at your mate, you must not permit it to continue. Your mate may be wrong, too opinionated, or way off base, but you can discuss that later. Joining the crowd against him will only make him feel like he is surrounded by a pack of wild dogs, and his defensive mechanism will automatically kick in.

Alone, in the privacy of your home—that is where you can talk about the problems you see. But remember, always get before the Lord prior to making any accusations or judgments. He will show you what the real problem is; and when He shows you the problem, He will also reveal the solution.

Father, *help me be a woman who handles problems with prayer, not with anger. Make me an everlasting wall of defense for my mate. Let my mate be reassured that no matter what comes at him, I will always have his back. I'm blessed that he's on my team. I pray for those who feel defenseless and afraid. Lord, let them know daily that they are special.*

63 DAY

Building Faith

Develop it now before the storms come.

And he did not many mighty works there
because of their unbelief.
—Matthew 13:58

Faith is somewhat like the chicken and the egg. What comes first? As for faith, when does it begin: in the saying or the doing or the done? For example: Say I ask you, "Do you think I can cross that raging river?" You might look at the water, then at me, and say, "Yes, I believe you can." What if I asked you, "Are you ready to get in the boat with me?" If your answer is no, your faith did not begin with the saying. It is easy to say you have faith, until you really need it. Now let's change perspective. If I look at a raging river and think, "I believe I can cross that river," when does my faith actually start? Is it when I say I believe? Is it when I get to the other side of the river that I truly believe? Or is it my belief that gets me into that boat? It is important that we recognize true faith, so we can build it.

Jesus, the Son of God, did not perform many mighty miracles in His own hometown because of the people's unbelief, which shows what an important part our belief plays in the whole scope

of the Lord's activity in our lives. Let's go deeper into the area of faith. You are going to need this in the coming days, so listen very closely.

Though faith is intangible, it's really very evident. Faith is believing that God will do what He has said he will do, and then acting on that belief. Faith is the saying, the doing, and the done.

How strong is your faith when it comes to overcoming problems, sickness, and discouragement? If you find yourself cowering at molehills, then you will never climb mountains. If you run from obstacles, then you will never get to where you dream of going. Will you chop off the heads of your personal Goliaths, or will you slink back in defeat?

Perform a faith checkup: How's your faith doing? Give yourself some credit. Now extend your faith a few more weeks. Can you see yourself on your honeymoon; do you smell the coconut lotion and feel the warm sun baking your tired bones? Your faith has just taken you through the raging waters of wedding preparation and to the calm waters of rejoicing in a job well done.

Father, *thank You for developing a strong faith in me. I know it will carry me through the storms of life, and I have the assurance of Your Word that I will come out on the other side. Help me believe in myself and in Your power, which resonates inside of me.*

Week Ten

• *Wedding Tips* •

Checklist: Ask your maid of honor to join you for your final gown fitting so she will know how to bustle your dress. Have your gown pressed, and bring it home. Make sure bridesmaids have their dresses ready. Check with your vendors. Make up gift bags for out-of-town guests, begin seating chart, review RSVP list, and call those who have not responded. Give your song list to the music director, and get your prewedding haircut/hair coloring.

• • •

Here are some ideas for items to carry on your wedding day: your and/or your mate's baby bracelets, your grandma's Bible, your mom's promise ring or pearls, a swatch from mom's wedding dress, or a few braided threads from your baby blanket.

DAY 64

ARE YOU LOSING YOUR SPACE?

Choose a gatekeeper.

And it came to pass, when Joseph was come unto his brethren, that they stript Joseph out of his coat, his coat of many colours that was on him; And they took him, and cast him into a pit.

—Genesis 37:23–24

Talk about losing some space! Joseph's brothers encroached on his space, stripped him of his prize coat, and changed his life's plans. You may be feeling some encroachment into your own well-defined space. We all have a comfort zone, physically and mentally.

The irritation you feel may be coming from all the wedding preparations, as you constantly fight to stay on track with your plans. People are invading your space, picking at your thoughts, and questioning your decisions. Your teeth are gritted, and it takes everything you have to get one thing accomplished in the manner in which you want it done. You want the votive candle placed in the center of each place setting, and every time you look, someone has decided it would look better to the right of the setting. As you snatch the votive candle and again place it in the center of the setting, you begin to breathe fire. With a threatening voice, you vow to slap the hand that touches that candle one more time.

When you multiply that scenario by a hundred for the many decisions you must make and defend, you can see why you are feeling encroached upon. How can you handle this situation and still remain a lady? First of all, put down that stun gun. That's an immediate solution for intruding hands, but we're looking for a more dignified approach. Put one of your dearest friends in charge of carrying out your requests; then if anyone has a problem with what you want done, you can refer that person to her. Tell those who question this that she's your wedding planner, and her job is to make sure that your plans and preferences are carried out correctly.

She will take all the heat from everyone, and she will also defend your space like an armed marine. In the business world, we call these smiling warriors *gatekeepers*. This may be radical, but out-of-control situations require drastic means. Now breathe!

Father, *thank You for friends and the ability to react wisely. I ask Your wise counsel as to who should be my gatekeeper. I need some breathing room, and I know You always have a solution for every problem. I look forward to shifting some of this pressure onto someone else who is willing to share my burden.*

Thoughts on My Helpers

DAY 65

DON'T LEAVE YOUR LIFE BEHIND

Chick flicks don't have to be a thing of the past!

David said to Saul,... "Your servant has killed both the lion and the bear; this uncircumcised Philistine will be like one of them, because he has defied the armies of the living God. The LORD who delivered me from the paw of the lion and the paw of the bear will deliver me from the hand of this Philistine." Saul said to David, "Go, and the LORD be with you."

—1 Samuel 17:34, 36–37 (NIV)

You're getting married, not falling off the face of the earth. A lot of familiar things you enjoy doing will still continue—I promise. You don't have to leave your friends behind, nor should you. You and your mate will soon become one in the spirit, but you are not surgically joined at the hip. Wipe those tears away. You shall once again blubber your way through *Titanic* with double-buttered popcorn.

It is important you don't leave behind the little things you do that make you happy. Let's face it: there are some things you are never going to get your hubby to enjoy. All the prayers in the world might not put a smile on your man's face as he waits for you to make one more trip to the fitting room. You don't have to do *everything* together. Why would you even think about walking away from the precious pieces of a life you so artfully crafted and molded?

You have invested a lot of yourself into you friends. They hold your precious secrets, have the knack for cheering you up

when you're down, and know which flavor of ice cream will bring a smile to your face.

Still, there is plenty of room for your mate to jump in anytime, and together, you will create your own special, intimate nuances. See how your life just gets richer and richer? Some will say you can't have it all, but that is not what our God says. You can still watch *Titanic* and, yes, throw in *Father of the Bride* while you're at it. But here's where it gets good. While you are out shopping, at the movies, or lunching with the girls, your mate is having some breathing time of his own. Then when you both come together, a renewing of the relationship takes place.

Your hobbies, passions, and interests cannot be left at the altar. These are all gifts you received from the Lord, and they are part of who you are. If you try to walk away from friends and the things of life you enjoy, even with that handsome man by your side, you will begin to experience a void. This commitment is for expansion—you're not signing up for a total makeover!

Father, *just as You designed David's life—from the first stepping-stone of being a shepherd boy to the giant step of becoming a king—prepare me for my destiny. Show me how to make all the pieces of my past fit into the picture you have created for my life.*

Thoughts of Times with Friends

66 · DAY ·

ESTABLISHING A PRAYERFUL MIND-SET

Silence is golden and prayer is platinum.

And the LORD said unto him, I have heard thy prayer and thy supplication, that thou hast made before me: I have hallowed this house, which thou hast built, to put my name there for ever; and mine eyes and mine heart shall be there perpetually.

—1 Kings 9:3

The stress is mounting as you near your big day. Decisions need to be made on a daily basis, emotions are escalating, and you've got almost three more weeks to go! If you don't begin your day with prayer, you will find yourself spinning like a top, turning into a hyperventilating nut. You know what I'm talking about. Your voice begins to raise a few notches, you develop a little tick in your right eye, and you keep spasmodically twisting your hair around your middle finger.

The way you take charge of your situation is through prayer. Before you pray, you must stop—stop thinking about RSVPs, the caterer, and the mounting bills. You do not have the power to change yesterday, but you do have the ability to change today. It is simply a mind-set. You tell your flesh what it is going to do, what it is going to eat, and how it will behave; do the same with your mind. Remember, David said, "Bless the LORD, O my soul: and all that is within me, bless his holy name" (Psalm 103:1). He

might not have been having the greatest of days, yet he told his whole being it was going to praise the Lord.

The power of your will and mind is surprising. It is possible to take control of your thoughts and out-of-control emotions if you take the time to get into the right frame of mind. Tell your loved ones you need some time alone. They will understand. Lock yourself up in the bathroom and take a long hot bath or go for a walk—do anything you like, as long as it puts distance between you and others.

There will be times in the future when you must be able to seek the face of God *in a split second*. You must keep yourself ready; you must maintain a prayerful mind-set. All those electronic gadgets blasting around you have off switches for a purpose—to turn them off. So do it…right now! Ahhhhhhhh. Do you hear the quiet? Yes, hear the silence. Feel your heart beat. Awaken your senses. Now you are prepared to pray.

Father, *just give me some plain old help. I don't know how I'm supposed to calm down in the midst of all this chaos. But this I do know: You are here with me. As long as You are here, then all is right with the world. Help me establish a prayerful mind-set to keep me looking to you first for counsel.*

Thoughts on This Quiet Moment

67 · DAY ·

GUARDING YOUR THOUGHTS

Who's that bully talking to you?

And when he putteth forth his own sheep, he goeth before them, and the sheep follow him: for they know his voice. And a stranger will they not follow, but will flee from him: for they know not the voice of strangers.

—John 10:4–5

Are you having fun yet? Remember, your wedding is supposed to be a happy, joyful event. What happened? Have worries and the what-ifs taken control of your thoughts? The Bible states, "as he thinketh in his heart, so is he" (Proverbs 23:7). So what have you been thinking? Have you ever noticed how worried thoughts come with a voice and a presence? You only have to read the Word to know that voice cannot possibly be the Lord's.

Anxiety and worry are accompanied by a heavy feeling, one that drains your energy and leaves you feeling exhausted. We know that when the Lord speaks, His voice brings strength and encouragement. So from where do you suppose all those heavy thoughts are coming: you know, the ones telling you it's going to rain on your wedding day, the colors you picked are all wrong, you look fat, your hair is going to frizz, and your mate doesn't really care about you? You know these thoughts are not from the Lord, so you've got to get control of them. But how?

Take each thought captive to the obedience of Christ (see 2 Corinthians 10:5) and replace it with prayer. When thoughts bring confusion and anxiety, laugh at them. You are going to have a wedding, and a fantastic one at that. Being anxious will not change one thing, but prayer will change *everything*. Being a Christian gives you another level of support the world does not have, nor does it understand. It gives you access to the throne room of God and the ability to call upon a power greater than yourself and mightier than any situation.

Tell that bully who's been talking to you, filling your head with all kinds of doubts and fear, to be gone, just like Jesus did (see Matthew 4:10). You *know* the voice of the one you follow, and it does not come laden with guilt or condemnation. When that condemning voice keeps yapping at you like an incessant dog barking and negative thoughts fire as rapidly as a machine gun, take control. Put a smile on your face. Believe that everything is going to be all right, and swat those unwelcome, annoying thoughts away as if they were irritating flies.

Father, *I love You. May my thoughts be of Your goodness, Your ability to make my dreams come true, and Your delight in me. Help me to recognize the different voices that speak to me; give me the wisdom to decipher which one is Yours and which ones are of the world.*

Thoughts on Recognizing God's Voice

DAY 68

Can You Make It?

How tenacious are you?

My righteousness I hold fast, and will not let it go: my heart shall not reproach me so long as I live.

—Job 27:6

Well, it's finally starting to come together. Mom's voice is getting dimmer. Auntie Mabel has stonewalled; yes, she is going to wear that awful orange dress, and you have accepted that fact. You haven't had a nervous breakdown. You've stopped gorging on double-fudge ice cream, and at the last fitting, you fit into your fabulous wedding dress. All is well.

Putting together a wedding is somewhat like sewing a quilt. Each piece has a special meaning that evokes certain feelings the maker wants to capture and give substance to. In its early stages, the quilt, to a casual observer, just looks like little scraps being put together with no rhyme or reason. The design, the intricate pattern, the planned outcome only the sewer knows. As the quilt reaches completion, the tiny, careful stitches reveal that this creation requires extreme patience and a willingness to labor, with only a vision to carry the maker through the long tedious task.

Your wedding vision is also unique in that you are the only one who sees it from the beginning to the end. You want to capture moments—highlighting some and embellishing others—to make some lasting memories. Do you have the patience and tenacity to carry out your intricate wedding plans? You have attended to each detail, seeking excellence in every area, from the coloring on your invitations to the placement of dainty baby's breath in your centerpieces. You're into the details, and that's OK.

Take a look at nature. Have you ever noticed the fragile fingernails on a baby or the delicate veins of a leaf? These are examples of God's detail work, created to bring a sense of wonder to those who partake.

You are also creating something: a magical day for those you love. You could elope, but then you'd miss the look on your mom's face as she sees you standing poised, elegant, and breathtaking in your wedding dress. You wouldn't feel that warm embrace as your father gives you one more hug. So yes, it is all worth it…as long as you remember one thing—the purpose. The creator of the quilt made it for a purpose: every stitch was sewn with the thought of blessing her loved ones long after she was gone. Don't lose sight of why you are creating this wonderful day.

Father, *help me to not lose sight of what this whole process is about. Let those who share in this wonderful day feel special and honored. If Your presence is there, then I know I will have accomplished all I set out to do. I pray for those who have become discouraged, having no dreams to keep them going. Please send someone in their path to bring them love, warmth, and hope.*

THOUGHTS OF WHAT'S REALLY IMPORTANT

DAY 69

YOU'RE GETTING IN DEEPER

Don't sandbag just yet.

Therefore I say unto you, What things soever ye desire,
when ye pray, believe that ye receive them,
and ye shall have them.
—Mark 11:24

This is really going to happen. You are getting married. All the things you desired are coming into place. But did you ever think you would feel like you do right now? Where's the joy...the bliss? Pressure, pressure, pressure. Your treasures are being packed up, you are signing checks large enough to alleviate the national debt, and now your intended wants to put his student loan under both your names. What are you getting into?

Some quirks are beginning to get your attention. You never noticed his mom calls him five times a day. Could this be a problem? How could you have overlooked the fact that he is a pack rat? Will you be buried alive under mounds of magazines? What were you thinking? He wants to convert one room in your two-bedroom flat into a gym. What is *he* thinking? Will this union ever work?

Are you being bombarded with worrisome thoughts? You are in a heightened state of anxiousness. His actions have now

convinced you, Inspector Clouseau, that he just might be an axe murderer.

Calm down. Think about it a moment. If he is the one the Lord has intended for you, then he must be your perfect complement. Forget about how he constantly drums his fingers on tabletops. Just accept that he is the one, because you asked God early in this process to confirm that fact, and He did. Trust in God, who knows you better than you know yourself. He caused your paths to cross. Consider the intricate planning and timing the Lord enacted to bring the two of you together. It is quite overwhelming!

What you are experiencing is fear, and you know fear is not of the Lord. Who can be fearful when they are laughing and in love? So keep the laughter and love flowing. The water's rising, but put down that sandbag; you might throw out your back! You don't want to be wobbling down the aisle in pain. Instead, reach for God's hand; He'll pull you out of this flood of anxiety and set your feet on solid ground.

Father, *as is too often the case, I have strayed from what I know to be true. I need to get back to basics. Lead me through a quick refresher: trust, love, peace, prayer, courage, integrity, and faith. Help me to get grounded once again. Thank You for another day.*

DAY 70

WHO'S THE BOSS?

It doesn't have to be a tug-of-war.

For the body is not one member, but many. If the foot shall say, Because I am not the hand, I am not of the body; is it therefore not of the body? And if the ear shall say, Because I am not the eye, I am not of the body; is it therefore not of the body?

—1 Corinthians 12:14–16

God runs a tight ship. Throughout the Bible, you see instances in which He has described how we can best work together to keep things running smoothly. That usually requires some kind of submission from everyone involved (see Ephesians 5:21). Unfortunately, it is inherent in most of us to want to rule over others.

Your married life will include many large and small decisions. If you want it to remain strong, you will learn to make decisions together based on input from your husband, you, and most importantly, the Lord. God desires your new family to be a healthy, happy, holy, functioning unit, and He will guide you toward that. It's like a body, in which all the members are needed and respected.

Before you both start competing for the position of boss, you might want to look down the road. Are you willing to be accountable to the Lord for all the bloopers that will occur in your marriage? Can you imagine the resentment you would feel

if your spouse-to-be tried to lord it over you without considering your needs and wants? The Lord is the head of your marriage, and He is constantly giving directives on what He wants done. He has given both of you gifts and skills that He wants you to use for the good of your marriage. He believes in you and the abilities you possess, and He fully expects you to run your lives with wisdom, sound judgment, and insight.

Respect one another's opinions. Counsel together, and you will not have to make a decision as to who's the boss. Keep in mind that you are now one in the spirit. Give the Lord the reins to your marriage, and you two can just sit back and enjoy the ride.

Father, *I am in awe of Your wisdom, and I bow my knee to Your authority. When I become too pushy or aggressive, give me a gentle tug. Hopefully, I will feel that bit in my mouth. Help me to let go of the reins of my life and learn to follow Your lead.*

WEEK ELEVEN

• *Wedding Tips* •

Checklist: Notify caterer of guest count. Break in wedding shoes at home. Confirm honeymoon arrangements. Make special boxes for people responsible for carrying important items, such as marriage certificate, copy of reception lease, and thank-you envelopes for band, drivers, and caterers. Give keys, instructions, and contact numbers to whoever will be tending your home (pets, plants) while you are on your honeymoon.

• • •

Contract wisdom: Look for the one-week rule, which means you may incur extra costs if you don't finalize all details seven days prior to your wedding. Also look for statements regarding liability insurance. If small vendors do not carry their own insurance, think about adding a rider to your existing homeowner's or renter's policy.

Losing Yourself?

It's temporary. You're right around the corner.

For thy mercy is great above the heavens: and thy truth reacheth unto the clouds. Be thou exalted, O God, above the heavens: and thy glory above all the earth.

—Psalms 108:4–5

Settle down. You are not lost; you are just buried under a mound of wedding tasks. Let's jot down what you are involved with, and maybe you will get a clearer picture of what's going on.

Over the last couple of months, you have been trying to lose ten pounds, plan a small Broadway production, arrange a vacation honeymoon, and set up housing arrangements. Your emotions are dealing with the fact that you will be acquiring another set of parents and siblings, abdicating your side of the bed, and assuming a new identity. Your pocketbook is in crisis mode because it knows it will have to share its already meager income, and it is currently feeling pinched from the wedding expenses.

Hello under there! Can you still hear me from under that mound? You may feel that it has been months since you've seen daylight, tasted your food, or felt a loving touch. You're in hyper mode, and you're spinning faster than a top. You are missing

the you that, during your preengagement days, would stop for a moment to observe God's creation. Enjoying His handiwork, an exquisite kaleidoscope of color spread out for your pleasure, is what kept you grounded, because it made you feel a part of something bigger than yourself. You've had to become so fragmented to pull off this wedding that you've gotten a little lost along the way.

The you that took time to enjoy God is still there, and the wonderful thing is that the choices are all yours. You can choose this day to be quiet for a moment and listen to the birds singing; you can look at the beautiful sky and watch as God paints a brilliant sunset; you can take time to touch a blade of grass or smell a sweet flower…and be in awe of Him.

Your heart hasn't gotten lost; it's just been temporarily diverted.

Father, *thank You for such an awesome world. Today I want to praise You and acknowledge Your handiwork. If what I see in the world is any sign of the preparation You've made for my wedding, then I realize, You have everything under control.*

Thoughts of God's Majesty

A Love Like Solomon's

He's got Brad Pitt beat, hands down.

Thy lips, O my spouse, drop as the honeycomb: honey and milk are under thy tongue; and the smell of thy garments is like the smell of Lebanon.

—Song of Solomon 4:11

Through a wide-angle lens, Brad Pitt may look great on the screen, and he may sound genuine as poetic phrases spill out of his mouth, but in reality, he's a created image designed to meet the needs of his adoring audience. Someone is writing those fantastic scripts, and someone else is capturing Brad's best look with just the right lighting. That's where the substance is—behind the scenes.

Your man may not have the cheekbones of a god, but how about that smile of his? He may not be able to turn heads, but he's got one good head on his shoulders. The power of love is in seeing beyond the package into the hidden man of the heart.

To have a man caress you with words, as Solomon did his love, is to have the heart of that man. When you can dig deeply into your love's mind and he pours out to you his secret hopes and fears, then you are on your way to experiencing pure, intimate love.

The Bible is a blueprint designed by the Lord to give us standards to live by. He shows us all that is possible for man to achieve, and He gives us insight into the plan He has for love between a man and a woman.

It is possible to have a love so rich that your heart flutters when your love enters a room or you hear his voice. Solomon loved so deeply he even talks of the scent of his love's garments.

A mysterious chemistry exists between lovers. When the Lord brings a man and woman together, He gives them each the key to unlock the other's soul. When two souls have access to one another, a pouring forth from one into another takes place. When you are feeling down, he gets you laughing. When he is discouraged, you speak words of hope and encouragement to him. This give-and-take is an intimate, beautiful ebb and flow between two lovers. Over time, it will become so fine-tuned that you can tell exactly how he feels by a minute shift in an eyebrow or a hesitation in his voice.

Don't forget who's premiering in this wedding production with you. Your love may have gotten a little overlooked over the past few months, but if you dig through all those weddings gifts and push aside those mounds of crinoline, I think you'll find him patiently waiting. Call to him. Like Solomon's love, he will hear and move heaven and earth to get to you.

Father, *please give me the gift of love and the wisdom to always recognize its value. May I never demean the price it comes with, and may I always seek entrance into the soul of the one I love. Thank You for giving me the keys to my love's heart.*

Thoughts on the Intimacies We Share

DAY 73

DON'T LEAVE YOUR LIFE BEHIND

Stay true to yourself. That's the woman he loves.

But God commendeth his love toward us, in that, while we were yet sinners, Christ died for us.

—Romans 5:8

Christ died for you and loves you for who you are. He accepts you as you are and deems you worth the price He paid. That is unconditional love. Many people miss this and continue striving for the day when they will be righteous enough for the Lord. While they are trying to achieve this impossible state, they miss the divine fellowship and friendship the Lord has for them.

The Lord began to love you a long time ago. Yes, He loves that woman who snaps her gum, loses her temper, and can't resist shoe sales. In fact, you probably bring Him quite a bit of amusement. In this world where people try so hard to be religiously correct, they lose sight of God's whole message—love.

Your intended also fell in love with you and everything about you. Well, maybe he could do without that control issue you have, but yes, he loves the total package, and that package includes girly nights that maintain your sanity and keep your

emotions from exploding. You need to continue having those special times. If you are a family person, then your family is your strength and support, and this will still be needed even though you are married. However, the parameters of your confidentiality with them will change because you now have a partner to share with. The makeup of who you are stems from *all* the components of your life.

You may have to curtail those shopping expeditions a bit, and you may lose that familiarity with the checkout girls, but your man loves the womanly side of you that can't pass up a bargain. He may get a little aggravated at you taking over the closet, but he loves the way you look in those cute T-shirts.

There is life after marriage, and if you allow the Lord to have a hand in it, your life will grow and expand. Making the transition from a single woman to a wife will be a little rocky, but with the Lord directing your footsteps, you won't miss a step.

We read in the Bible that we are to love our neighbors as ourselves (Matthew 22:39), but here's a message we seldom hear, yet one that is essential: Love ourselves as our neighbors. Take the liberty of loving yourself and all the Lord has created within you. You are lovable right where you are, as you are!

Father, *help me to love myself. Let me rejoice in all I am. Give me the wonderment of a child at the miraculous work You have done in me. Give me the capacity to walk in the wholeness and totality of complete love for myself, my mate, and those You place in my path.*

• DAY 74 •

ALIEN AFFECTIONS

Maybe he hasn't had his caffe latte yet.

And Jesus went into the temple of God, and cast out all them that sold and bought in the temple, and overthrew the tables of the moneychangers, and the seats of them that sold doves.

—Matthew 21:12

Jesus was a man of great temperance, patience, and love, but He did get angry at times, as you can see in the Scripture above. Since it was not generally His nature to react in anger, we need to look for the motive that stirred up that reaction. The money changers were providing Jewish coins in exchange for the foreign coins of those who had come from afar to worship in Jerusalem, and in the process, the money changers were defrauding the unsuspecting people. For that, and perhaps other reasons, Jesus experienced indignation, a righteous anger.

You know the nature of the man you love, and if he behaves a little differently than normal, look for the driving force behind the change. Take time to be sensitive to his needs, which may have been left by the wayside among all the wedding preparations. Maybe he is feeling a little distant from you, left out, and irritated with all the goings-on, or it might be he just doesn't understand what's so important about each little detail of this

wedding. Whatever the issue is, his feelings are important enough for you to stop what you are doing and try to resolve the problem. Don't fall into the trap of reacting to his moodiness with silence, sulking, or temper tantrums. Pray for guidance from the Lord.

We all have up and down days, and certain issues can pull our chains, ignite our passions, and call forth the warrior inside of us. Throughout your married life, you will find that from time to time, simple little things may cause you to slam doors and stomp out of rooms. You will also discover a better way, through prayer and a deeper walk with Christ, and He will lead you to it.

Your alien mate will transform into your Prince Charming on the day of your wedding, so bear with him. Realize he hasn't gone anywhere; he may just be hanging out on the sidelines, observing all the wedding preparations. Your mate loves you; that's a given. Now, step back, take a deep breath, and give him room to vent. If that doesn't work, forget the high-octane espresso and move on to relaxing comfort foods. Put a warm cup of cocoa in his hands, snuggle up with him, and just hang on till the storm passes.

Father, *thank You for Jesus and the life He led as an example for all of us. Seeing the human side of divinity lets me know You do understand the emotions we experience. Help me to be one who strives for peace, because "Blessed are the peacemakers: for they shall be called the children of God."**

*See Matthew 5:9.

THOUGHTS ON WHAT MAKES HIM TICK

DAY 75

FORGIVENESS

To go forward, let go of the past.

But if ye forgive not men their trespasses, neither will your Father forgive your trespasses.

—Matthew 6:15

As a society, we have lots of ways to get rid of junk. We have erasers, delete buttons, yard sales, garbage cans, and trusty old matches. Sometimes things we do are just plain wrong, mistakes, or belong to yesterday, and we want to move on and set everything straight. The Lord, in His wisdom, provided our souls with a great big purge button called *forgiveness*.

If you are carrying around old grudges, harboring resentment toward others, or feeling bitter inside, get rid of that debris. It can blur your vision, harden your heart, and blind you to what the Lord has for you.

Picture your soul as a blackboard. All those tiny chalk marks representing your past junk actions don't seem like much, but when you step back and look at the board, it is filled with items you thought were long gone. Get out your spiritual eraser, *prayer,* and ask forgiveness from the Lord and, if appropriate, from those whose names are printed on that board.

Forgiveness brings a tremendous sense of freedom, cleanliness, and refreshment. Do you remember the delightful feeling you had when you were born again, knowing you were cleansed from all sins, righteous before the Lord, and totally spotless? That sensation is available to you every day.

You don't want to walk into your new life dragging a bag of junk with you. Today is the day to unload all that junk you have been carrying and lighten your load. Begin with the one you love. Forgiveness is granted through loving actions, gentle hugs, and the hardest words to say in the English language, "I'm sorry." The Lord has so empowered these words that saying them makes you huge in the eyes of those to whom you say them. These kind, simple words can reduce a grown man to tears and melt any bitterness in a relationship. They have the energy to bring restoration to broken friendships and mend wounded hearts.

When you ask God for forgiveness, He puts your sins as far away as the east is from the west, and He sees them no more. Since you are His daughter, He expects the same kind of latitude from you toward others.

Father, *I want to be cleansed today. Forgive me for the sins I have committed. Grant me the ability to move in forgiveness toward others. May it serve me all through my life and be a standard that I live by. I never want to go to sleep with unforgiveness separating me from You.*

Thoughts of Forgiveness

DAY 76

TRUST THE LORD

He's an A-1 wedding planner.

And wheresoever he shall go in, say ye to the goodman of the house, The Master saith, Where is the guestchamber, where I shall eat the passover with my disciples? And he will shew you a large upper room furnished and prepared: there make ready for us.

—Mark 14:14–15

The above Scripture shows how Jesus had a plan in motion for one Passover celebration way before His disciples first thought about it. (See Mark 14:12–16.) This gives us a snapshot of Jesus and how He moved and operated. The day was planned, the room reserved, and the event prepared. Do you think He is any less skilled today at orchestrating a wedding for you? I think not!

You cannot control the weather, traffic, flights, flowers blooming, cakes rising, or people, so you might was well relax and go take a nap. After you have logically done all you can do and prepared to the best of your ability, the moment comes for you to say, "It is done."

You are so close to the finish line. You see it is all coming together, and you should feel some pressure releasing. You have reached that pivotal point where everything is set in motion and what will be, will be. Like a mother giving birth, once the real

contractions begin, that baby is coming! Your dream is about to be born. You will waltz down the aisle in your fantasy dress, those you love will be there to witness your commitment to your chosen mate, and all of your hard work will finally culminate into a wonderful day for everyone.

At this point, you must trust the Lord. If things go awry, just realize there may be a purpose in it. You can't see it now, but years from now when you look back, it may all make sense.

These last couple of days should be devoted to pampering yourself. Many customs allow weeks to prepare the bride for her wedding. Today, brides scurry around like bees on a pollen high and then think a one-hour massage before the wedding will knead out all their stress. Forget about the aisle runner. Look at yourself! You need to get a manicure, a pedicure, and maybe some tanning, and it might be time to start conditioning that hair. Seriously, take some time for yourself. Your guests will be just fine.

Father, *I could not have made it through this and kept my sanity without You. I want to take some quiet time to give You thanks and listen for Your voice. Show Yourself as the great I Am, the Restorer to those who have lost faith in themselves.*

THOUGHTS ON PREPARING FOR MY WEDDING

DAY 77

Moving into His Heart

Don't bring too much baggage.

Keep thy heart with all diligence;
for out of it are the issues of life.
—Proverbs 4:23

When you are preparing to move into a new place, the first thing you do is scrub it clean, put a fresh coat of paint on the walls, and remove any signs of the previous tenants. Because you want to make it your own, you wipe away its "memories" of prior residents.

The spirit of a man, his core being, lives in his heart. Over the years, your man's heart has accumulated many things that cannot and should not be discarded. Memories paper the walls of his soul, and cherished moments are stacked up for him to relish at his leisure. These are things from his past, of which you were not a part.

You can't move in and expect him to throw out his treasures as though they are trash. It is easy to be jealous of things that don't include you. Not all intimate moments can be shared; some are meant to be held close solely by the person who experiences them. Your man has memories with his family and friends that you will never share, and you must respect that. You can't expect his heart

to be swept clean upon your arrival. But don't worry about that; if you look, you will find he has made a huge space just for you.

Your two hearts will be merged as only the Lord can do. It's a God thing. This thing called love makes scientists scratch their heads and psychologists go nuts, because they can't explain it, pointing once again to the mysteries of God.

So how do two hearts become one and still allow enough room for both people to live comfortably while holding on to treasured memories? Do both of you have to let go of memories held so dear, or close your minds to treasured thoughts, never to bring them to the light of day again? Why, no!

Blue is a beautiful color that stands on its own, and so is vibrant red. When the two are mixed, they become a third color, purple. Neither color gives up its original function or pigment, but when mixed with the other color, a change takes place and a new exciting color is formed. The same can be said of your relationship. Individually, you both are fantastic; together, you are phenomenal.

As you step over the threshold into his heart, tread very lightly. His memories are hung haphazardly on the walls of his heart, and his collectible moments may be strewn all over, but he knows the location of every one of them. You have no idea how much preparation and cleaning he has already done to welcome you in, so accept his heart's hospitality. If he trusts you enough, he might even give you a private tour into the hidden rooms of his heart.

Father, *give me the wisdom to step back when I need to and the ability to acknowledge the fact that I am not my love's entire world. You created him for Your pleasure. I thank You for the honor of being chosen to share his heart.*

THOUGHTS ON MY LOVE'S PAST

Week Twelve

• *Wedding Tips* •

Checklist: Assign people to specific duties, such as distributing corsages, delivering gift bags to hotel, and so on. Assign a family member to be the photographer's contact. Remind groom to get his hair trimmed. Determine wedding party positions during the ceremony. Deliver welcome baskets to the hotel concierge. Write checks, and see about final balances. Pack an emergency bag for your wedding day. Pack for honeymoon. Attend bachelorette party. Clear up last-minute details at work. Have a manicure and pedicure. Attend your rehearsal dinner, and present attendants with gifts.

• • •

Give wedding bands to the best man and maid of honor. Give the best man the officiant's fee. Present parents with gifts. Now, no more to-do lists! Relax and enjoy the festivities.

DAY 78

It Is All Coming Together

So take a day off.

And Moses said unto the people, Fear ye not, stand still, and see the salvation of the LORD, which he will shew to you to day: for the Egyptians whom ye have seen to day, ye shall see them again no more for ever.

—Exodus 14:13

Take note of a key phrase in the Scripture above: "stand still, and see the salvation of the LORD." Why don't you do that today? Stand still for a moment, and look behind you. Now look where you are today. Pictures of wedding dresses torn out of bridal magazines have been relegated to the garbage as you look at your exquisite gown weighing down its padded hanger. Ideas that started out with swatches of material have now materialized into bridesmaid dresses. Tons of wedding invitation samples were done away with months ago, as you stuffed your delicate invitations into creamy envelopes and placed on those "too cute" postage stamps.

All the worry, anxiety, and indecision are dispelling as you approach your special day. Hindsight is always better than foresight, of course; isn't it easy now to step back and say, "What in the world was all the fuss about?" You wanted to create a unique day for yourself, your mate, and those you love, and you have

accomplished that, and kept a smile on your face...most of the days. This week will end in a moment of triumph. Give yourself a pat on the back...or at least one scoop of chocolate chip cookie dough ice cream.

You're nearing the finish line, and the road behind you doesn't look all that bad today. Like with childbirth, you will forget the pain during the moment of celebration. Was all your pain worth your gain? Was the fuss justified? Only you will be able to answer that—and only after your wedding day is past. But I have a feeling you will find you wouldn't have had it any other way. It's the whole process that creates a wedding, and that process naturally produces some worry, irritation, and frustration. A wedding just wouldn't come to fruition without some of that.

For generations, women have labored over this process. It's a rite, a ritual that abounds in womanhood, moves you toward wifehood, and ends when the lights go out at your reception hall. Our society accepts and welcomes this ritual because it puts an enchanting detour in our ordinary lives and, for just a time, moves us all into the dreamworld of blushing brides, innocent love, and idealistic futures. So enjoy this day. You have worked hard to get here!

Father, *thank You for a day off. Give me supernatural peace, and lift from me any heaviness I feel. Fill my heart with love and joy for my mate, and let the whole earth rejoice because I am in love!*

THOUGHTS FOR MY DAY OFF!

DAY 79

DO THIS RIGHT

He doesn't come with a warranty.

Jesus said unto him, Thou shalt love the L*ORD thy God with all thy heart, and with all thy soul, and with all thy mind.*

—Matthew 22:37

I know you have been in situations in which you have had only one shot at getting something right. It could have been a graduation at which you would walk down that aisle only once or maybe an important competition in which you had just one shot to give your best performance.

In each instance, you had only one chance to capture the moment, to crystallize it in time. When you understood you were under the gun to perform, having prepared yourself, you found yourself operating at a high level of excellence. You left little margin for error, having gone over and over in your mind your plan for achieving your goal. Do you remember your heightened state of anticipation?

Why was this so important to you? It was because you understood the importance of getting it right *the first time.* You knew there would not be a second opportunity. If you will apply this same idea to your marriage, you will have a successful partnership.

Don't approach this union as one that has options, such as, "If it doesn't work out, we can just get divorced."

In life, when options exist, apathy is more prevalent. What do I mean by that? Choice is good, you may tell me, and I agree. Being able to choose between nonfat fudgesicles and Häagen-Dazs ice cream is a no-brainer. But when we are talking about the lifetime commitment of marriage, your choice was made when you agreed to marry this man.

Approach each day with your mate as if it were a once-in-a-lifetime occurrence, because, in reality, it is. You will never have this day back to try to create wonderful memories, so do it this one time through. You will never be able to relive your day to take back hurtful words or erase angry looks, so avoid such things as you live out each day.

Your mate doesn't come with a warranty stating he will always work right, always say the proper things, and never malfunction. But with your wedding vows, you should offer him your guarantee that you will stay by his side, no matter what the future holds. Accept the gift he is to you from the Lord, and strive to always treasure the moments you share. And yes, that even includes moments when you want to return him to his Maker.

Father, *I'm striving for excellence. Let me never fall into a state in which my vision of life gets cloudy and I lose the ability to hold life as a precious gift. My mate was given to me from You, and that is all the warranty I need.*

· DAY 80 ·

IF YOU HEAR THE WORD *WEDDING* ONE MORE TIME...

Hold on! You're almost there.

And the children of Israel did eat manna forty years, until they came to a land inhabited; they did eat manna, until they came unto the borders of the land of Canaan.

—Exodus 16:35

In Exodus 16, the Israelites complained about not having any food to eat. Read the whole chapter, and you will see how the Lord handled murmuring and complaining. He rained so much manna and quail down upon the people that they were swimming in it. Don't you know, too much of a good thing can make you sick? When you were a child, did you ever want something so bad, like chocolate cake, and then eat so much of it that it made you sick?

Your wedding began as such a fun thing to do, and now it has totally consumed your life. You are having to deal with too much cake, lace, and baby's breath and, now, too many people. What started out as a labor of love has birthed itself into a two-headed monster, and the pain is not over quite yet. At this point, your thoughts may be of taking flight, eloping, or riding off into the sunset with your man. Who gives a hoot about the music anyway? At this point, you'd be willing to dance a jig

down the aisle with tiny munchkins singing, "Follow the yellow brick road."

Hold on! You're almost there. You've just been snacking too long on that manna and quail. How about some lean cuisine today? Just *something* different—and you'll be good to go. The frustration you feel is that of a woman who is anxious to get on with her life. Making wedding plans was fun for a while, but now you want to taste its fruit.

You yearn for the days when you had time to think about or do things other than planning a wedding. Those days are coming; they're just not here yet. What you are experiencing is normal. When a person is overwhelmed, the first response is to run, hide, or escape, but unless you want to make the news as a runaway bride, you have to gird yourself up with prayer. The Lord sees your situation and is ready to help. He'll maneuver you through the next couple of days. You will find milk and honey on the other side, beginning with the honeymoon.

Father, *please still my mind, and put a guard on my lips. I am about to scream, and I feel I have gotten into waters too deep for me. I'm sinking fast! If You don't hold me up, You will find me drowned in a sea of lace, lilies, and table linens. Help!*

THOUGHTS FOR MAKING IT THROUGH THE DAY

DAY 81

You're Ready

That walk down the aisle is getting shorter.

Again, he sent forth other servants, saying, Tell them which are bidden, Behold, I have prepared my dinner: my oxen and my fatlings are killed, and all things are ready: come unto the marriage.

—Matthew 22:4

You are ready. Everything is prepared, and it's time for a celebration. Months ago, did you ever think you would, or could, go through such a whirlwind of emotions? You've come a long way from that hushed bridal salon where you first stepped into your dress. Remember the lights in the salon, the sight of your veil cascading over your hair, and the way you felt as that dress floated over your body, puddling at your feet?

In a few days, you are going to don that gown for real and command the attention of a roomful of people. All eyes will be on you; your every move will be carefully watched, but not in a way that makes you feel self-conscious. When those doors open and you appear, you will be opening up pages of memory books, nestled in the minds of the married women present; every one of them will drift back in time, once again, to their own weddings. The little girls will be dreaming of their future weddings when they see you, and fathers will get melancholy, as thoughts begin

to stir of how one day they will be walking their own daughters down an aisle. Your walk down the aisle will seem like an eternity to you, but those in attendance will silently wish for you to move a little slower, so they can enjoy their memories a few moments longer. And you thought it was all about you. Surprise!

A bride symbolizes life going on and the spirit of humanity's refusal to give up on the greatest gift of all—love. You, as the bride, are the embodiment of all that is hopeful, fresh, and new. Your shimmering veil hides the glowing countenance of a woman who trusts in the transition from the innocence of a child to a woman. The hushed oohs and aahs are the reverence guests feel as they see the bride and are awed and befuddled to see that even tomboys turn into regal princesses and plain Janes into radiant women when dressed in love and excited anticipation on their wedding day.

Father, *thank You for taking time with me—all the time I needed—to help me get through the past few months. Your grace has always been extended toward me. I ask for Your arm as I walk down the aisle. Please be there beside me, and never let me fall.*

• DAY •

You've Changed

What was once tapioca is now crème brûlée.

Then David arose from the earth, and washed, and anointed himself, and changed his apparel, and came into the house of the LORD, and worshipped: then he came to his own house; and when he required, they set bread before him, and he did eat.

—2 Samuel 12:20

Can you remember eating instant tapioca as a child? Something about rolling those tiny bumps over your tongue just brought happiness. Now crème brûlée takes you to a sophisticated level of taste that somehow signifies you have arrived. This creamy, rich custard is enhanced by the brittle, caramelized, sugary topping created by applying heat or fire to it, thereby, making it a dessert of contrasts—just like your life.

Whether you are a smart businesswoman, an industrious college student, or a love-struck high school graduate, you are about to enter the secret world of married women. It's an exciting step in your life. This covert world has been in existence since the beginning of time, and it holds a cluster of women who have taken on the responsibilities of making new lives, raising families, and creating nests in which they can grow old with their mates.

This world of married women is characterized by change, movement, and progression. Look how far you have come from

that magical day your beloved asked you to be his bride. All those bumps in the road are gone, and all your complex wedding details have ironed out into a beautifully planned wedding. One day you are flouncing around the fitting room in your crinoline—laughing as you plop down and your crinoline flies up, enveloping your head—and what seems like just a few days later, you will be regally moving down the aisle with your crinoline swaying to the strains of "Here Comes the Bride."

Yes, in a couple of days, you will marry. The Lord has perfected many changes in your heart and soul. Your prayers over the last couple of months have not been just empty words whispered into the wind; your pleas have reached the ears of the Lord, and He is ever faithful to honor the requests of His servants. You are now sophistication personified. So gracefully put down that candy bar, and daintily pick up your spoon. Take a big bite out of life, and savor the taste. Ahhhhhhhh, sophistication is so smooth.

Father, *thank You for working and believing in me. You have guided my footsteps over the bumpy roads of wedding planning and have made my feet to glide upon paths laden with promises, joy, and anticipation. I love the excitement of knowing You always have something new for me, and I pray for the willingness to always be ready to change.*

DAY 83

"Abba, Don't Leave Me Now"

"I need You!"

For ye have not received the spirit of bondage again to fear;
but ye have received the Spirit of adoption,
whereby we cry, Abba, Father.

—Romans 8:15

Everything is set, all your plans are coming together. Family and friends have gathered, and it's time to celebrate. Take a deep breath. Just months ago, hundreds of decisions loomed in front of you, and you really didn't know whether you could pull this wedding off. But you've done it; it is really happening.

Dozens of relationships have changed, expanded, and deepened as you neared this final week. Your love is holding his breath, counting the minutes until he can whisk you away and have you all to himself. Your mom is looking forward to waking up without wedding details constantly marching through her head, and your friends can't wait to go out to lunch with you and discuss something besides your wedding plans. Yes, this is true. But that's OK; you're the bride! Relish this time and hold on to it.

Fear may raise its ugly head, and you may envision toppled wedding cakes, wilted flowers, and walking down the aisle with your dress wedged into your panty hose, but take comfort in the

fact that you are not alone. You've got a special Someone pulling for you—a Father whom you can call Abba, which means Daddy—and He has the power to make everything all right. He wants you to enjoy all that He has prepared for you. You are blessed. Don't forget that.

Months ago, you gave this whole production into His hands. Today is not the day to take it back. What He started, He is well able to finish. He's not the Alpha and Omega for nothing!

It's hard to trust the Lord looking forward, but if you look behind you, you see His work clearly. You can see moments lit up like tiny fireflies: times He was constantly intervening, setting things right, and creating joy. Close your eyes. I know you are very busy today, but just take a second to be still before the Lord. Can you feel His power all around you? Be aware of His presence, warm and soothing, like a tranquil summer rain. Do you sense His excitement? He's ready to walk you down the aisle, and with Him at your side, there is absolutely no chance of failure or mishap. It's time to celebrate!

Father, *thank You for Your presence. You told me, "do not fear, for I am with you,"* and I will listen to Your voice. Help my love and me enjoy this celebratory gathering of family and loved ones. I place myself—spirit, soul, and body—into Your open arms, and I relish this special moment You and I are having. I will carry it with me all through the day.*

*Isaiah 41:10 (NIV)

THOUGHTS OF GOD'S FAITHFULNESS

DAY 84

COVENANT

To have and to hold forever—that's our promise.

Now therefore come thou, let us make a covenant, I and thou; and let it be for a witness between me and thee.

—Genesis 31:44

You are just hours away from stepping into that gorgeous gown. You're primped, powdered, and polished to within an inch of your life. Upon your bed lies your filmy veil, dainty garter, and frilly crinoline. Voices are shouting throughout your house, cell phones are ringing, and the doorbell keeps chiming. A couple of rooms away, your bridesmaids are giggling, jostling all of your presents, and Auntie Mabel is snoozing in the chair. Your dad is pacing the floor, your mom is running around tending to last-minute details, and your love is somewhere being ministered to by his best man.

Take a moment to quiet your thoughts and realize the magnitude of this day. You are about to enter into a covenant with the Lord and the man you love. The Lord will bind the two of you together and expect you to honor your vows and commitments to one another. Your mate is entrusting his life, his dreams, and his soul to you; understand this is no small thing.

Can you be there when he is sick, destitute, lacking hope, and faithless? Are you strong enough and willing enough to be his other half, his complement?

Life is a gift from the Lord, and being able to share it with the one you love is the bow on the package. Make a vow to always put your mate's needs above yours, and you will never lack; put his dreams above yours, and you will always succeed; put his love above all others, and you will never be alone. One day you and your mate will meet in heaven. You will transcend this earthly realm and enter the domain of the living God. All you have ever done will be laid out before you. May it be a life of love, happiness, and giving. What greater reward could there be than to stand before the King of kings with your mate, heads bowed, as He tells you, "Well done, my faithful servants"?

Well, that's enough seriousness. This is your day, girl! You're walking down that aisle into the arms of the man you love, and yes, you have made the right decision.

See? I told you everything was going to be just fine. This day I'd like the honor of praying a blessing over you.

May your marriage stand the test of time and life itself. May you know the gift of true love and have the endurance to keep that love untouched by the world. May you never know lack. I pray the Word blesses you beyond measure. May you love one another forever and hold to each other throughout eternity. There's only one thing left to say. I speak these golden prophetic words over your fairy-tale life:

"And they lived happily ever after!"

Thoughts to Remember on My Wedding Day

New Hope® Publishers is a division of WMU®,
an international organization
that challenges Christian believers to understand
and be radically involved in God's mission.
For more information about WMU, go to www.wmu.com.
More information about New Hope books
may be found at www.newhopepublishers.com.
New Hope books may be purchased at your local bookstore.

After Your *Wedding* You May Enjoy

Love Notes on His Pillow
And Other Everyday Ways to Keep Your Love Alive
Linda J. Gilden
ISBN 1-59669-014-3

Famous Lovers in the Bible
And Marriage-Building Secrets We Learn from Their Relationships
Doug and BJ Jensen
ISBN 1-56309-810-5

When the Glass Slipper Doesn't Fit
Claire Cloninger and Karla Worley
ISBN 1-56309-437-1